BUTOH

Books LLC®, Wiki Series, Memphis, USA, 2011. ISBN: 9781156905197. www.booksllc.net
Copyright: http://creativecommons.org/licenses/by-sa/3.0/deed.en

Table of Contents

Butoh
Akaji Maro 1
Butoh... 2
Edoheart 4
Kazuo Ohno 6
Keiji Haino 7
Simona Orinska 9
Tadashi Endo 10

Butoh dance companies
DEREVO 10

Kokoro Dance 10
Sankai Juku 11

Sopor Aeternus
A Strange Thing To Say 12
Dead Lovers' Sarabande (Face One) 12
Dead Lovers' Sarabande (Face Two) 13
Ehjeh Ascher Ehjeh 13
Es reiten die Toten so schnell 14
Es reiten die Toten so schnell... 14
Flowers in Formaldehyde 15

Ich töte mich...................................... 15
La Chambre D'Echo 16
Like a Corpse standing in Desperation 17
Sanatorium Altrosa 18
Songs from the Inverted Womb 19
Sopor Æternus & the Ensemble of Shadows 19
The Inexperienced Spiral Traveller... 22
Todeswunsch 23
Voyager: The Jugglers of Jusa 24

Introduction

Purchase of this book entitles you to a free trial membership in the publisher's book club at www.booksllc.net. (Time limited offer.) Simply enter the barcode number from the back cover onto the membership form. The book club entitles you to select from hundreds of thousands of books at no additional charge. You can also download a digital copy of this and related books to read on the go. Simply enter the title or subject onto the search form to find them.

Each chapter in this book ends with a URL to a hyperlinked online version. Type the URL exactly as it appears. If you change the URL's capitalization it won't work. Use the online version to access related pages, websites, footnotes, tables, color photos, updates. Click the version history tab to see the chapter's contributors. Click the edit link to suggest changes.

A large and diverse editor base collaboratively wrote the book, not a single author. After a long process of discussion and debate, the chapters gradually took on a neutral point of view reached through consensus. Additional editors expanded and contributed to chapters striving to achieve balance and comprehensive coverage. This reduced the regional or cultural bias found in many other books and provided access and breadth on subject matter otherwise little documented.

Akaji Maro

Akaji Maro (麿 赤児 *Maro Akaji*, born February 23, 1943) is a Japanese actor, Butoka, and theater director. He was born in Sakurai, Nara and is the founder of Dairakudakan. His son is Nao Ōmori.

Selected filmography

Film
- *Sakigake!! Otokojuku* (2008)
- *Makai Tensho* (2003)

- *Kill Bill Vol. 1* (2003)
- *Kikujiro* (1999)
- *Cat's Eye* (1997)
- *Yamato Takeru* (1994)
- *Yumeji* (1991)
- *Shinran: Path to Purity* (1987)
- *Burst City* (1982)
- *Yaju-deka* (1982)
- *Kagero-za* (1981)
- *Zigeunerweisen* (1980)

Television
- *Kindaichi Case Files* (1996)
- *Psychometrer Eiji* (1997)
- *GARO* (2006)
- *Yamada Tarō Monogatari* (2007)
- *Atsuhime* (2008)

Source (edited): "http://en.wikipedia.org/wiki/Akaji_Maro"

Butoh

Gyohei Zaitsu performing Butoh

Butoh (舞踏 *Butō*) is the collective name for a diverse range of activities, techniques and motivations for dance, performance, or movement inspired by the **Ankoku-Butoh** (暗黒舞踏 *ankoku butō*) movement. It typically involves playful and grotesque imagery, taboo topics, extreme or absurd environments, and is traditionally performed in white body makeup with slow hyper-controlled motion, with or without an audience. There is no set style, and it may be purely conceptual with no movement at all. Its origins have been attributed to Japanese dance legends Tatsumi Hijikata and Kazuo Ohno.

History

Butoh appeared first in Japan following World War II and specifically after student riots. The roles of authority were now subject to challenge and subversion. It also appeared as a reaction against the contemporary dance scene in Japan, which Hijikata felt was based on the one hand on imitating the West and on the other on imitating the Noh. He critiqued the current state of dance as overly superficial.

The first butoh piece, *Kinjiki (Forbidden Colours)* by Tatsumi Hijikata, premiered at a dance festival in 1959. It was based on the novel of the same name by Yukio Mishima. It explored the taboos of homosexuality and paedophilia and ended with a live chicken being held between the legs of Kazuo Ohno's son Yoshito Ohno, after which Hijikata chased Yoshito off the stage in darkness. Mainly as a result of the misconception that the chicken had died due to strangulation, this piece outraged the audience and resulted in the banning of Hijikata from the festival, establishing him as an iconoclast.

The earliest butoh performances were called (in English) "Dance Experience." In the early 1960s, Hijikata used the term "Ankoku-Buyou" (暗黒舞踊 – dance of darkness) to describe his dance. He later changed the word "buyo," filled with associations of Japanese classical dance, to "butoh," a long-discarded word for dance that originally meant European ballroom dancing.

In later work, Hijikata continued to subvert conventional notions of dance. Inspired by writers such as Yukio Mishima (as noted above), Lautréamont, Artaud, Genet and de Sade, he delved into grotesquerie, darkness, and decay. At the same time, Hijikata explored the transmutation of the human body into other forms, such as those of animals. He also developed a poetic and surreal choreographic language, *butoh-fu* (舞踏譜) (*fu* means "notation" in Japanese), to help the dancer transform into other states of being.

The work developed beginning in 1960 by Kazuo Ohno with Tatsumi Hijikata was the beginning of what now is regarded as "butoh." In Jean Viala's and Nourit Masson-Sekinea's book *Shades of Darkness*, Ohno is regarded as "the soul of butoh," while Hijikata is seen as "the architect of butoh." Hijikata and Ohno later developed their own styles of teaching. Students of each style went on to create different groups such as Sankai Juku, a Japanese dance troupe well-known to fans in North America.

Students of these two great artists have been known to highlight the differing orientations of their masters. While Hijikata was a fearsome technician of the nervous system influencing input strategies and artists working in groups, Ohno is thought of as a more natural, individual, and nurturing figure who influenced solo artists.

Debate

There is much discussion about who should receive the credit for creating butoh. As artists worked to create new art in all disciplines after World War II, Japanese artists and thinkers emerged out of economic and social challenges that produced an energy and renewal of artists, dancers, painters, musicians, writers, and all other artists.

A number of people with few formal connections to Hijikata began to call their own idiosyncratic dance "butoh." Among these are Iwana Masaki (岩名雅紀), Tanaka Min (田中民), and Teru Goi. Although all manner of systematic thinking about butoh dance can be found, perhaps Iwana Masaki most accurately sums up the variety of butoh styles:

While 'Ankoku Butoh' can be said to have possessed a very precise method and philosophy (perhaps it could be called 'inherited butoh'), I regard present day butoh as a 'tendency' that depends not only on Hijikata's philosophical legacy but also on the development of new and diverse modes of expression. The 'tendency' that I speak of involved extricating the pure life which is dormant in our bodies.

Hijikata is often quoted saying what opposition he had to a codified dance: "Since I believe neither in a dance teaching method nor in controlling movement, I do not teach in this manner." However, in the pursuit and development of his own work, it is only natural that a "Hijikata" style of working and, therefore, a "method" emerged. Both Mikami Kayo and Maro Akaji have stated that Hijikata exhorted his disciples to not imitate his own dance when they left to create their own butoh dance groups. If this is the case, then his words make sense: There are as many types of butoh as there are butoh choreographers.

Starting in the early 1980s, butoh experienced a renaissance as butoh groups began performing outside Japan for the first time. The most famous of these groups is Sankai Juku. During one performance by Sankai Juku, in which the performers hung upside down from ropes from a tall building in Seattle, Washington, one of the ropes broke, resulting in the death of a performer. The footage was played on national news, and butoh became more widely known in America through the tragedy. A PBS documentary of a butoh performance in a cave with no audience further broadened knowledge in America.

In the early 1990s, Koichi Tamano performed atop the giant drum of San Francisco Taiko Dojo inside Grace Cathedral, in an international religious celebration.

Butoh's status at present is ambiguous. Accepted as a performance art overseas, it remains fairly unknown in Japan.

Butoh in popular culture

A Butoh performance choreographed by Yoshito Ohno appears at the beginning of the Tokyo section of Hal Hartley's 1995 film *Flirt*.

Ron Fricke's experimental documentary film *Baraka* (1992) features scenes of butoh performance.

In the late 1960s, exploitation film director Teruo Ishii hired Hijikata to play the role of a Doctor Moreau-like reclusive mad scientist in his film horror movie *Horrors of Malformed Men*. The role was mostly performed as dance. The film has remained largely unseen in Japan for forty years because it was viewed as insensitive to the handicapped.

Kiyoshi Kurosawa used butoh movement for actors in his 2001 film *Kairo*, remade in Hollywood in 2006 as *Pulse*. The re-make did not feature butoh.

Butoh performance features heavily in Doris Dörrie's 2008 film *Cherry Blossoms*, in which a Bavarian widower embarks on a journey to Japan to grieve for his late wife and develop an understanding of this performance style for which she had held a life-long fascination.

A portrait of Kazuo Ohno appears on the cover of the 2009 Antony & the Johnsons album *The Crying Light*.

Butoh has greatly influenced the Sopor Aeternus and the Ensemble of Shadows, the musical project of Anna-Varney Cantodea. Its visual motifs are used in for the project's publicity photos and videos.

Initial butoh dancers

Hijikata's female principal dancer was Yoko Ashikawa. Ashikawa lives in Japan. She no longer makes public performances.

Yukio Waguri was a young student in the last company of Tatsumi Hijikata. Waguri still lives in Japan, teaches, and performs all over the world.

Another principal dancer for Hijikata was Koichi Tamano. Tamano made his United States debut in 1976 at the "Japan Now" exhibition at the San Francisco Museum of Modern Art. Hijikata called Tamano "the bow-legged Nijinsky," a quote later rendered in English by Allen Ginsberg.

Ko Murobushi was responsible for bringing butoh to Europe in the 1970s. He and Akaji Maro started the company Dairakudakan in Tokyo.

Butoh exercises

Most butoh exercises use image work to varying degrees: from the razorblades and insects of Ankoku Butoh, to Dairakudakan's threads and water jets, to Seiryukai's rod in the body. There is a general trend toward the body as "being moved," from an internal or external source, rather than consciously moving a body part. A certain element of "control vs. uncontrol" is present through many of the exercises.

Looked at from completely scientific standpoint, this is rarely possible unless under great duress or pain but, as Kurihara points out, pain, starvation, and sleep deprivation were all part of life under Hijikata's method, which may have helped the dancers access a movement space where the movement cues had terrific power. It is also worth noting that Hijikata's movement cues are, in general, much more visceral and complicated than anything else since.

Most exercises from Japan (with the exception of much of Ohno Kazuo's work) have specific body shapes or general postures assigned to them, while almost none of the exercises from Western butoh dancers have specific shapes. This seems to point to a general trend in the West that butoh is not seen as specific movement cues with shapes assigned to them such as Ankoku Butoh or Dairakudakan's technique work, but rather that butoh is a certain state of mind or feeling that influences the body directly or indirectly.

Hijikata did in fact stress feeling through form in his dance, saying, "Life catches up with form," which in no way suggests that his dance was mere form. Ohno, though, comes from the other direction: "Form comes of itself, only insofar as there is a spiritual content to begin with."

The trend toward form is apparent in several Japanese dance groups, who merely recycle Hijikata's shapes and present butoh that is mere body-shapes and choreography which would lead butoh closer to contemporary dance or performance art than anything else. A good example of this is Torifune Butohsha's recent works.

A paragraph from butoh dancer Iwana Masaki, whose work shies away from all elements of choreography.
I have never heard of a butoh dancer entering a competition. Every butoh performance itself is an ultimate expression; there are not and cannot be second or third places. If butoh dancers were content with less than the ultimate, they would not be actually dancing butoh, for real butoh, like real life itself, cannot be given rankings.

Defining butoh

Critic Mark Holborn has written that butoh is defined by its very evasion of definition. The *Kyoto Journal* variably categorizes butoh as dance, theater, "kitchen," or "seditious act." The *San Francisco Examiner* describes butoh as "unclassifiable". The *SF Weekly* article "The Bizarre World of Butoh" was about former sushi restaurant Country Station, in which Koichi Tamano was "chef" and Hiroko Tamano "manager". The article begins, "There's a dirty corner of Mission Street, where a sushi restaurant called Country Station shares space with hoodlums and homeless drunks, a restaurant so camouflaged by dark and filth it easily escapes notice. But when the restaurant is full and bustling, there is a kind of theater that happens inside…" Butoh frequently occurs in areas of extremes of the human condition, such as skid rows, or extreme physical environments, such as a cave with no audience, remote Japanese cemetery, or hanging by ropes from a skyscraper in front of the Washington Monument.

Hiroko Tamano considers modeling for artists to be butoh, in which she poses in "impossible" positions held for hours, which she calls "*really* slow Butoh". The Tamano's home seconds as a "dance" studio, with any room or portion of yard potentially used. When a completely new student arrived for a workshop in 1989 and found a chaotic simultaneous photo shoot, dress rehearsal for a performance at Berkeley's Zellerbach Hall, workshop, costume making session, lunch, chat, and newspaper interview, all "choreographed" into one event by Tamano, she ordered the student, in broken English, "Do interview." The new student was interviewed, without informing the reporter that the student had no knowledge what butoh was. The improvised information was published, "defining" butoh for the area public. Tamano then informed the student that the interview itself was butoh, and that was the lesson. Such "seditious acts," or pranks in the context of chaos, are butoh.

Influence

Teachers influenced by more Hijikata style approaches tend to use highly elaborate visualizations that can be highly mimetic, theatrical and expressive. A good example of this teaching would be Koichi and Hiroko Tamano, founders of Harupin-Ha Butoh Dance Company (who own and operate the Tamasei Sushi restaurant in San Francisco).

Teachers who have spent time with Ohno seem to be much more eclectic and individual in approach, bearing the mark of their master, perhaps, in tendencies to indulge in wistful states of spiritualized semi-embodiment.

There have been many unique groups and performance companies influenced by the movements created by Hijikata and Ohno, ranging from the highly minimalist of Sankai Juku to very theatrically explosive and carnivalesque performance of groups like Dairakudakan.

International

Street butoh performance in Seattle, Washington, USA

Many Nikkei (or members of the Japanese diaspora), such as Japanese Canadians Jay Hirabayashi of Kokoro Dance, Denise Fujiwara, incorporate butoh in their dance or have launched butoh dance troupes.

Butoh is also created and performed by non-Japanese Canadians – Thomas Anfield and Kevin Bergsma formed BUTOH-a-GO-GO in 1999 billing it a "Second Generation Butoh/Performance Company." Anfield and Bergsma met in 1995 working with Kokoro Dance.

The multimedia, physical theater-oriented group called Ink Boat in San Francisco incorporates humor into their work. Another San Francisco performance troupe, COLLAPSING*silence* was formed in 1992 by Terrance Graven, Indra Lowenstein, and Monique Motil. The group was active for 13 years and participated in The International Performance Art Festival in 1996. They often collaborated with live musicians such as Sharkbait, Hollow Earth, Haunted by Waters, and Mandible Chatter. The Swedish SU-EN Butoh Company tours Europe extensively. Another prominent butoh-influenced performers is the American dancer Maureen Fleming.

More notable European practitioners, who have worked with butoh and avoided the stereotyped 'butoh' languages which some European practitioners tend to adopt, take their work out of the sometimes closed world of 'touring butoh' and into the international dance and theatre scenes include Marie-Gabrielle Rotie, Kitt Johnson (Denmark) and Katharina Vogel (Switzerland). Such practitioners in Europe aim to go back to the original aims of Hijikata and Ohno and go beyond the tendency to imitate a ' master' and instead search within their own bodies and histories for 'the body that has not been robbed' (Hijikata).

Eseohe Arhebamen is the first African butoh performer and practices a style she calls "Butoh-vocal theatre".
Source (edited): "http://en.wikipedia.org/wiki/Butoh"

Edoheart

Eseohe Arhebamen also known as **Edoheart** (born **Obehioye Eseohe Ikhianose Oghomwenyenmwen Cleopatra Anne Arhebamen**) is a poet, dancer, singer, performance artist and visual artist. Eseohe was born in Zaria, Nigeria on April 9, 1981 and is descended from a royal family of the Benin Empire. Eseohe Arhebamen's great-grandfather Osazuwa Eredia was the Oba N'Ugu and enogie of Umoghumwun, making her a royal descendant and princess. "The foundation of the kingdom of Ugu, with its capital at Umoghumwun has been traced to

Prince Idu, the eldest son of Oba Eweka I."

Early life

Eseohe Arhebamen is the oldest of five siblings and frequently played a parental role in their upbringing. At the age of seven Eseohe's family immigrated to the United States and settled in Detroit, Michigan. At age 17 she enrolled in the University of Michigan at the Residential College. Although strongly encouraged to pursue medicine as a career path, Eseohe instead followed her passion for poetry, language and the arts. As an undergraduate student Eseohe focused on literary means and performance as a way to affect social change. While at the University of Michigan, Eseohe won prestigious awards for her writing and is included in a University of Michigan Anthology of Hopwood Award winners.

Career

At 19 years old, Eseohe earned a position as Writer-in-Residence with InsideOut Literary Arts Project in Detroit, Michigan and worked with children in impoverished inner-city schools to expand their literary skills. After moving to New York in 2003, Eseohe founded the company EdoHeart also written as Edoheart which became her performance name. Eseohe Arhebamen is synonymous with Edoheart.

Eseohe received her BA from the University of Michigan in Creative Writing and Literature in August, 2005, and went on to receive another BA in Studio Art with a minor in English from Hunter College. Eseohe also studied Butoh dance with Yukio Waguri.

Areas of interest in Eseohe Arhebamen's experimental work are imaginative creation of alternate environments, and poetry and vocal expressions as a source for movement. She has choreographed and taught or led workshops involving these areas of interest at The Living Theatre and Columbia University's Teacher's College. Eseohe Arhebamen has appeared on Korean television and news, and in American, Estonian and Latvian newspapers.

Butoh Vocal-Theatre Invention

Eseohe Arhebamen is the first performer to combine Japanese Butoh dance with singing, talking and experimental vocalizations. She refers to this dance style as Butoh-Vocal Theatre. Eseohe Arhebamen's Butoh-Vocal Theatre style arises out of her work in poetry, music and the traditional Edo theater in which performers dance and sing simultaneously and is influenced by her expressed belief in a common lingual history between the Edo people of Nigeria and the Japanese. On September 26, 2010 Eseohe gave a performance at a Yukio Waguri intensive workshop demonstrating her style of Butoh-Vocal Theatre during which she danced butoh while singing Pure Imagination from Willy Wonka & the Chocolate Factory.

Eseohe's notable performance during the Fifth Diverse Universe tour was described by Kaarel Kressa as embodying natural elegance and femininity; with poetry, dance and song that won the hearts of the audience. Eseohe's performances have also been called "powerful ritual".

Marriage

In 2006, Eseohe married long time sweetheart Seth Yamasaki, son of Pulitzer Prize winning photographer Taro Yamasaki, and grandson of Minoru Yamasaki, Japanese-American architect best known for designing the World Trade Center. The two live in Brooklyn, New York.

Poetry books

2010 Jesus of All Niggers, Poems 1998-2009 (Laughing Mouse Press)
   2003 Seeding the Clouds (Ornithology Press)

Discography

2010 Shchedryk Avant Remix (Clinical Archives)
   2010 Monsoon in Ibadan (Clinical Archives)
   2010 Wa Domo Edo (Edoheart)
   2009 The Hunger Artist (Eseohe)

Film and video

2009 Excerpt of Fire Butoh 3 for the Low Lives Exhibition
   2009 Blue Butterfly Butoh
   2009 The Cement Factory
   2009 #18 / Number 18
   2009 eAir Butoh Sketch
   2008 Fire Butoh 3 Visuals
   2008 Fire Butoh 3
   2008 Fire Butoh 2
   2008 Es Su Casa
   2007 Fire Butoh 1
   2007 The N Word

Anthologies and catalogues

2009 Diverse Universe Festival 2005-2009, Academia Gustaviana Selts Mty
   2009 Low Lives, Jorge Rojas
   2009 Kunsti Aastaraamat, Parnu Linnavalitsuse kultuuriosakond (Cultural Department of Parnu City Government), Printon Printing House
   2009 세계 실험예술의 메카, 홍대 앞 - 인터넷서점 인터파크도서
   2006 The Hopwood Awards: 75 Years of Prized Writing, University of Michigan Press
   2006 The New Spend Less Revolution, Harriman House

Awards

2006 Poet of the Day, Poets Against the War
   2002 Environmental Justice Initiative First Place Award, University of Michigan
   2002 College Unions Poetry Slam National Champion First Place, Ohio Invitational
   2000 Writer-in-Residence, InsideOut Literary/Arts Project
   2000 Arthur Miller Award (Fiction)
   2000 Jeffrey L. Weisberg Memorial Prize in Poetry
   2000 Hopwood Minor Poetry Award
   2000 Hopwood Underclassmen Fiction Award
   1998 Residential College Fellowship, University of Michigan
Source (edited): "http://en.wikipedia.org/wiki/Edoheart"

Kazuo Ohno

Kazuo Ohno (大野 一雄 *Ōno Kazuo*, October 27, 1906 – June 1, 2010) was a Japanese dancer who became a guru and inspirational figure in the dance form known as Butoh. It was written of him that his very presence was an "artistic fact."

He is the author of several books on Butoh, including *The Palace Soars through the Sky, Dessin, Words of Workshop,* and *Food for the Soul.* The latter two were published in English as *Kazuo Ohno's World: From Without & Within* (2004).

Ohno once said of his work: "The best thing someone can say to me is that while watching my performance they began to cry. It is not important to understand what I am doing; perhaps it is better if they don't understand, but just respond to the dance."

Early life

The son of a fisherman and a mother who was an expert in European cuisine, Ohno was born in Hakodate City, Hokkaido Prefecture, Japan, on October 27 in 1906. He demonstrated an aptitude for athletics in junior high school and graduated from an athletic college in 1929, teaching physical education at a Christian high school. In 1933, Ohno began studying with Japanese modern dance pioneers Baku Ishii and Takaya Eguchi, which qualified him to teach dance at the Soshin Girls' School in Yokohama (from where he retired in 1980.)

In 1938, Ohno was drafted into the Japanese Army as a lieutenant, and later rose to captain. He fought in China and New Guinea, where he was captured and interned by the Australians as a POW. The war and its horrors provided him with inspiration for some of his later works, such as *Jellyfish Dance*, thought to be a meditation on the burials at sea he had observed on board the ship transporting soldiers back to Japan.

Career

After the war, he began work on his dance again, and presented his first solo works in 1949 in Tokyo. In the 1950s, he met Tatsumi Hijikata, who inspired him to begin cultivating Butoh, a new form of dance evolving in the turmoil of Japan's drab postwar landscape. Hijikata, who rejected the Western dance forms popular at the time, developed with Ohno and a collective group the vocabulary of movements and ideas that later, in 1961, he named the Ankoku Butoh-ha movement.

During the 1960s, Ohno sought his own style, while collaborating with Tatusmi Hijikata. In 1977, he premiered his solo *La Argentina Sho* [Admiring La Argentina], directed by Hijikata and dedicated to the famed Spanish dancer Antonia Mercé (known as "La Argentina," whom he had seen perform in 1926.) He received Japan's prestigious Dance Critics' Circle Award for the performance and subsequently toured the piece, impacting the international dance world from the 14th International Festival at Nancy, France, in 1980, to his American debut in 1981 at La MaMa Experimental Theatre Club in New York City. Other cities on the tour included Strasbourg, London, Stuttgart, Paris and Stockholm.

With Hijikata directing, Ohno created two more major works, *My Mother* and *Dead Sea*, performed with his son, Yoshito Ohno. Other works include *Water Lilies, Ka Cho Fu Getsu'* [Flowers-Birds-Wind-Moon] and *The Road in Heaven, The Road in Earth*. He was awarded a cultural award from Kanagawa Prefecture in 1993, a cultural award from Yokohama city in 1998, and the Michelangelo Antonioni Award for the Arts in 1999.

Teaching

Ohno established the Kazuo Ohno Dance Studio in 1949, and built the Kamihoshikawa studio in 1961 in Hodogaya, Yokohama, for the creation and rehearsal of his choreography. Now under the aegis of son Yoshito Ohno, the Kazuo Ohno Dance Studio conducts workshops, produces performances and has established a butoh archive, collecting and classifying all materials related to butoh and Kazuo Ohno's legacy. Ohno's studio is currently open for students to attend. Classes are directed by Yoshito.

Personal life

A devout Baptist since his conversion as a young man, Ohno supported himself through much of his life as a physical education teacher at Kanto Gakuin High School, a private Christian school in Yokohama from where he retired at 86.

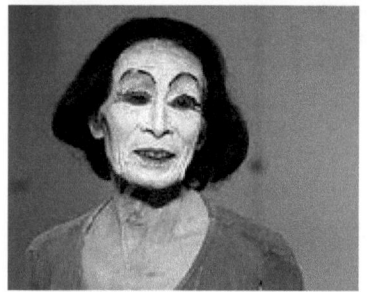

In October 1986

Ohno starred in the films *O-shi no shozo* [A Portrait of Mr. O] (1969) directed by Chiaki Nagano *The Scene of the Soul* (1991) by Katsumi Hirano; and the documentary *Kazuo Ohno* (1995), directed by Daniel Schmid. He wrote three books on Butoh, including *The Palace Soars through the Sky*, a collection of essays and photographs; *Dessin* with drawings and notes on his Butoh creations; *Words of Workshop*, a collection of lectures given in his workshop; and *Food for the Soul*, a selection of photography from 1930's through 1999. The latter two books were combined and published in English as *Kazuo Ohno's World: From Without & Within* (2004, Wesleyan University Press). In October 2006, soon after Ohno's 100th birthday, Kyoto-based publisher Seigensha released a photography book in homage to Ohno featuring the works of Eikoh Hosoe entitled *The Butterfly Dream*.

He is featured on the cover of Antony and the Johnsons' 2009 CD *The Crying*

Light.

Later years and death

In 2001, though he lost his ability to walk, Ohno continued performing and developed ways to express himself through dance solely by moving his hands. In recent years, Ohno had been under nurse's care at home, but he continued his stage appearances, particularly in the butoh works of his son Yoshito Ohno. In January 2007, he made his final public appearance in Yoshito's Hyakkaryoran at a gala celebrating his 100th birthday. He died of respiratory failure on June 1, 2010, at 4:38 pm (JST), in Japan at the Yokohama Senin Hoken Hospital in Yokohama City, at the age of 103.

Source (edited): "http://en.wikipedia.org/wiki/Kazuo_Ohno"

Keiji Haino

Keiji Haino (灰野 敬二 *Haino Keiji*) born May 3, 1952 in Chiba, Japan, and currently residing in Tokyo, is a Japanese musician whose work has included rock, free improvisation, noise, singer-songwriter, solo percussion, psychedelic, minimalism and drone styles. He has been active since the 1970s and continues to record regularly and in new styles.

History

Haino's initial artistic outlet was theatre, inspired by the radical writings of Antonin Artaud. An epiphanic moment came when he heard The Doors' "When The Music's Over" and changed course towards music. After brief stints in a number of blues and experimental outfits, he formed improvised rock band Lost Aaraaf in 1970. In the mid 1970s, having left Lost Aaraaf, he collaborated with psychedelic multi-instrumentalist Magical Power Mako and film soundtrack composer Toru Takemitsu.

His musical output throughout the late 1970s is scarcely documented, until the formation of his rock duo Fushitsusha in 1978 (although their first LP did not surface until 1989). This outfit initially consisted of Haino on guitar and vocals, and Tamio Shiraishi on synthesizer. With the departure of Shiraishi and the addition of Jun Hamano (bass) and Shuhei Takashima (drums), Fushitsusha operated as a trio. The lineup soon changed, with Yasushi Ozawa (bass) and Jun Kosugi (drums) performing throughout the 1990s, but returned to a duo with Haino supplementing percussion with tape-loops.

Haino formed Aihiyo in 1998, principally playing a diverse range of covers (including The Rolling Stones, The Ronettes, and the Jimi Hendrix Experience), transforming the original material into Haino's unique form of garage psychedelia.

Other groups Haino has formed include Vajra (with underground folk singer Kan Mikami and drummer Toshiaki Ishizuka), Knead (with the avant-prog outfit Ruins), Sanhedolin (with Yoshida Tatsuya of Ruins and Mitsuru Nasuno of Altered States and Ground Zero) and a solo project called Nijiumu. He has also collaborated with a diverse range of artists, including Faust, Boris, Derek Bailey, Joey Baron, Peter Brötzmann, Lee Konitz, Loren Mazzacane Connors, Charles Gayle, Earl Kuck, Bill Laswell, Musica Transonic, Stephen O'Malley, Mikigami Koichi, Merzbow, Oren Ambarchi, Jim O'Rourke, John Zorn, Yamantaka Eye, John Duncan and Fred Frith.

Style

His main instruments of choice have been guitar and vocals, with many other instruments and approaches incorporated into his career's work. Haino is known for intensely cathartic sound explorations, and despite the fact that much of his work contains varied instrumentation and accompaniment, he retains a distinctive style.

Haino cites a broad range of influences, including troubadour music, Marlene Dietrich, Iannis Xenakis, Blue Cheer, Syd Barrett, and Charlie Parker. His recent foray into DJing at Tokyo nightclubs has reportedly reflected his eclectic taste. He has had a long love affair with early blues music, particularly the works of Blind Lemon Jefferson, and is heavily inspired by the Japanese musical concept of 'Ma', the silent spaces in music (see Taiko for more information). He also has a keen interest in Butoh dancing and collecting ethnic instruments.

Solo & Collaborative Discography

- Watashi Dake (1981)
- Kaii Abe (Collaboration with unknown musicians) (1982)
- Nijiumu (1990)
- Live in the first year of the Heisei, Volume One (With Kan Mikami and Motoharu Yoshizawa (1990)
- Live in the first year of the Heisei, Volume Two (With Kan Mikami and Motoharu Yoshizawa (1990)
- Live at Lazyways, Koenji, Tokyo (with Toshi Ishizuka) (1992)
- Itsukushimi (Affection)(1992)
- <live> 30 - June - 1992 (1992)
- Execration that accept to acknowledge (1993)
- Ama No Gawa (Milky Way) (1993)
- Guitar Works (7")(1994)
- Beginning and end, interwoven (1994)
- Hikari=Shi" (light=death) (Maki Miura, Keiji Haino, and Ogreish Organism) (1994)
- Two strings will do it (Barre Phillips, Keiji Haino, and Sabu Toyozumi) (1994)
- Live at Downtown Music Gallery (Keiji Haino and Loren Mazza Cane Connors) (1995)
- A Challenge to Fate (1995, reissued 2004)
- Tenshi No Gijinka (1995)
- I said, This is the son of nihilism (1995)
- Twenty-first Century Hard-y Guide-y Man (1995)
- Etchings in the air (Barre Phillips and Keiji Haino) (1996)
- Evolving Blush or Driving Original Sin (With Peter Brotzmann) (1996)

- Gerry Miles (With Alan Licht) (1996)
- The Book of "Eternity Set Aflame" (1996)
- Saying I love you, I continue to curse myself (1996)
- Drawing Close, Attuning—The Respective Signs of Order and Chaos (With Derek Bailey (1997)
- Vol. 2 (Keiji Haino and Loren Mazza Cane Connors) (1997)
- Keeping on breathing (April 21, 1997)
- Sruthi Box (Promotional Release) (April 21, 1997)
- So, black is myself (May 1, 1997)
- The 21st Century Hard-y Guide-y Man (1998)
- Incubation (with Musica Transonic) (1998)
- Black: Implication Flooding (With Boris) (1998)
- Even Now, Still I Think (June 24, 1998)
- An Unclear Trial: More Than This (With Greg Cohen and Joey Baron) (November 1998/January 1999)
- Y (With Jean-Francois Pauvros) (January 2000)
- The Strange Face (With Shoji Hano) (September 2000)
- Shadow - Live in Wels, Austria (With Shoji Hano & Peter Brotzmann) (September 2000)
- Ichioku to ichibanme no inori o michibiki daseba ii (With Coa) (October 2000) A translation: You should draw out the billion and first prayer
- Songs (With Derek Bailey) (December 2000)
- Abandon all words at a stroke, so that prayer can come spilling out (May 2001)
- Until Water Grasps Flame (With Yoshida Tatsuya) (January 2002)
- Mazu wa iro o nakusouka!! (Nov 5, 2002)
- Free Rock (Doo-Dooettes + Keiji Haino + Rick Potts) (Nov 25, 2002)
- "C'est parfait" endoctriné tu tombes la tête la première (January 2003)
- Hikari yami uchitokeaishi kono hibiki (December 24, 2003)
- Koko (December 24, 2003)
- Live at Cafe Independants Friday 23. January. 2004 (Keiji Haino, Tatsuya Yoshida & Mitsuru Natsuno + Bus Ratch) (June 2004)
- Tayu tayu to tadayoitamae kono furue (With Michihiro Sato) (July 2004)
- Next Let's Try Changing the Shape (April 2004, January 2005)
- Black Blues (soft version) (May 2004)
- Black Blues (violent version)(May 2004)
- Uchu Ni Karami Tsuite Iru Waga Itami (March 10, 2005)
- kono kehai fujirareteru hajimarini (August 25, 2005)
- Reveal'd to none as yet - an expedience to utterly vanish consciousness while still alive (December 2005)
- New Rap (With Yoshida Tatsuya) (March 2006)
- Homeogryllus japonicus Orchestra 2004 (With Mamoru Fujieda) (April 2006)
- Animamima (With Sitaar Tah!) (May 2006)
- Yaranai ga dekinai ni natte yuku (August 15, 2006)
- Mamono (With KK Null) (November 2006)
- Cosmic Debris, Vol.III (With My Cat Is An Alien) (August 2007)
- Uhrfasudhasdd (With Yoshida Tatsuya) (May 2008)
- Pulverized Purple (With Masami Akita) (July 2008)

Vajra
- Tsugaru (1995)
- Chiru-Ha/Ozakijinjya (CD-Single) (1995)
- Ring (1996)
- "Sichisiki" (The Seventh Consciousness) (1997)
- Sravaka (1998)
- Mandala Cat Last (2002)
- Live 2007 (2007)

Aihiyo
- untitled (1998)
- Second Album (2000)

Black Stage
- untitled (with Natsuki Kido & Yuji Katsui) (1996)

Purple Trap
- Soul's True Love (4CD) (1995)
- Decided... Already The Motionless Heart Of Tranquility, Tangling The Prayer Called "I" (1999)

Knead
- 1st (May 2002)
- This melting happiness - I want you to realize that it is another trap (July 2003)

Sanhedolin
- Manjoicchi wa muko (August 10, 2005)

Lost Aaraaff
- untitled (1991)

Nijiumu
- Era of Sad Wings (1993)
- Live (Part of Driftworks 4CD box-set)

Source (edited): "http://en.wikipedia.org/wiki/Keiji_Haino"

Simona Orinska

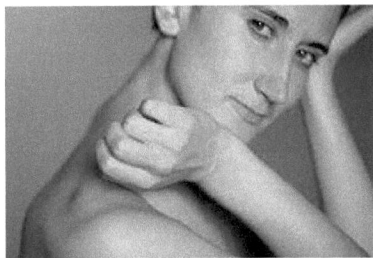

Simona Orinska

Simona Orinska (born August 18, 1978 in Ērgļi, Latvia) is the only butoh artist in Latvia and a multidisciplinary artist - contemporary dancer, poet, director and choreographer of many art projects. She is also a Dance Therapy or Dance Movement Therapy practitioner.

Background

Simona grew up in Ērgļi until she was about 6–7 years old, then her family moved to small village called Misa (Latvia). When she was 17 years old she moved to Riga and started her study in Riga Applied College. She studied in the Environmental Design Department specializing in Object Design from 1997 to 2000. Then from 2000 to 2005 she completed both her bachelor and master degrees in arts in Latvian Academy of Culture. Her passion in arts motivated her to complete her second master degree in Health Service and Art Therapist Professional Qualification with specialization in Dance Movement Therapy in the Riga Stradina University from 2006 to 2009.

Butoh career

Simona had her first exposure on butoh in a workshop with Sophie Cournede from Schloss Brölin Art Center, Germany way back in 2002. But she started actively engaging butoh only since 2005:

- 2005 Anita Saij butoh method (Nordic School of Butoh, Denmark)
- 2006 Susanna Akerlund butoh method (SU-EN butoh company, Sweden)
- 2007 Masterclasse with Ken Mai (Riga, Latvia)
- 2007 Butoh dance masterclasses with Ken Mai, Yukio Waguri, Tsuruyama ZULU Kinya (in the frameworks of Nonverbal Arts festival „Vertical 2007: Buto Relations", (Saint Petersburg, Russia)
- 2007 SU-EN butoh company workshop and participating in the international performance project „The Chicken project – Romeo and Juliet" (Sweden, Uppsala, Shakespeare's Festival,)
- 2007 KITT JOHNSON workshop „Expressive Anatomy" (Denmark)
- 2010 Swee Keong, Lai Chee (Malaysia, Kuala Lumpur, 2010 Nyoba Kan International Butoh Festival,)
- 2010 Joao Roberto de Souza (butoh artist from Brazil, in a workshop of 2010 Nyoba Kan International Butoh Festival, Kuala Lumpur, Malaysia)
- 2010 Toshiharu Kasai (stage name Itto Morita) (Japan), in a workshop

In 2008, she was involved in the International Arts Synergy Festival in Riga. She also made a multimedia performance butoh performance titled "Eyes Fluttering in My Knees."

In 2010, she will make a new performance titled "The Sacred Dances of the Night" at Happy Art Museum (www.pinakoteka.lv) in Riga, Latvia on October 30, November 6 & 27 together with Modris Tenisons (artist, director), Artis Gulbis (performance & sound artist), Gita Straustina(video artist), Skaidra Jančaite (Lithuania, singer), Ken Mai (Japan, co-author, consultant of performance), Ērika Māldere (artistic lighting designer) and her companion Aigars Lenkēvičs (graphic designer) from Lamp Design Worshop.

Other Dance Performances

Apart from butoh performances, she also involved in a processional art performance - "Somebody who leads" and a performance in a photo exhibition - "On Haiku". She also participated in an international video dance project (Latvia, England, Portugal, Spain, Chile, Hungary). Premiere was held in 2007, August 17 in the frameworks of the International Video Art Festival "Waterpieces 07".

Dance Movement Therapy

Simona is a private Dance Therapy or Dance Movement Therapy practitioner under the supervision of Medicine Association "ARS" (Medicīnas sabiedrība "ARS": http://www.ars-med.lv/start.php?lang=en). She provides both individual and group Dance Movement Therapy. Her clients consist of both children and adults. She uses movement to improve her clients' physical, emotional, cognitive and social capabilities. She uses this therapy to help her clients to ease emotional and physical stress, solve psychosomatic difficulties, garner life energy, obtain deep relaxation, develop creativity and feel the joy of body movement.

Simona complements the individual Dance Movement Therapy with the Champi ("filling with energy" in Sanskrit) massage, which is a type of Ayurvedic massages rooted in India. The Champi massage is based on the natural health care system of Ayurveda, which incorporates massage, yoga, meditation and herbal remedies (herbalism). Instead of traditional using ways of yoga and meditation, she uses the Dance Movement Therapy to give her clients a feeling of dynamic motion and inner peace, and uses the Champi massage to give her clients a feeling of full relaxation and external tranquility. She believes that the integration of these two therapies can have more wholesome therapeutic effect on her clients.

During the Champi massage, her clients will usually be asked to sit down. Then she will first massage her clients' shoulders, than their hands, necks and head zones. These step-by-step movements of massage will pressure her client's energetic lines and points and are strictly regimented. She also uses the aromatic essential oils of great value and finds every client specific oils matching her or his type.

Since April 20, 2009, she is employed as an art therapy specialist (Dance Movement therapist) in a children hospital "Gailezers" and works with children with psychiatric problems.

She had two Dance Movement Therapy internships in Bristol, the United Kingdom in 2008, namely in a dance movement therapy center called "Dance Voice" (client groups: mental health problems, addiction recovery, learning difficulties, autistic children and individual clients) and in a special school for autistic children called "St.Cristopher's School" (client groups: Individual clients with autistic spectrum disorders.

She was also one of the founding members of Latvian Dance Movement Therapy Association. She is now one of the members in the Board of Directors of the Association.
Source (edited): "http://en.wikipedia.org/wiki/Simona_Orinska"

Tadashi Endo

Tadashi Endo (born 1947) is a butoh dancer resident in Göttingen, Germany. Endo is a Japanese national. He studied theatre direction in Vienna before touring Europe giving solo performances accompanied by leading jazz performers. In 1980, he was hired as head of a theater program for the city of Northeim, where he worked until 1986. In 1992, founded the MAMU butoh center in the near-by university city of Göttingen. The center holds performances as well as training students of the dance form and holding an annual festival in the Goettingen Junges Theater. Endo also tours internationally. In 2009, he choreographed Georg Friedrich Händel's opera *Admeto*, directed by Doris Dörrie and performed at the Edinburgh International Festival.

Endo was greatly influenced by Kazuo Ohno, whom he met in 1989. Endo's style is harsh and stark, sometimes accompanied by live or recorded jazz, a dance form that Endo sees as having a natural affinity with butoh.
Source (edited): "http://en.wikipedia.org/wiki/Tadashi_Endo"

DEREVO

DEREVO is a physical theatre company inspired by Butoh founded by **Anton Adasinsky** in 1988 in St. Petersburg (former Leningrad), Russia, later in Prague, Czech Republic and now based in Dresden, Germany since 1996.

They have performed throughout Europe, Russia and the UK, as well as in the United States and at festivals in South Korea, Japan and Brazil. They have produced a 16 mm film *Süd. Grenze*, music CDs, photography books etc.

Founding members of DEREVO include: Anton Adasinsky (earlier he had been frontman, choreographer and played various instruments in the Soviet rock band AVIA and a member of Slava Polunin's pantomime theatre Litsedeyi); Tanya Khabarova; Dmitry Tyulpanov; Alexey Merkushev and Elena Yarovaya. DEREVO have collaborated with: Oleg Zhukovsky, Adam Read, Yael Karavan, Roman Dubinnikov (composer, percussionist, sound designer), Andrey Sizintsev (composer, percussionist, sound designer), Daniel Williams (composer, pianist/keyboards, sound designer), Falk Dittrich (lighting designer), Sergey Jakovsky (lighting designer).

Awards

DEREVO have received:
- Total Theatre Award, Fringe First, Herald Angel and Herald Archangel at the Edinburgh Festival Fringe
- Support prise for performing arts of Academy of Arts in Berlin
- Prix du Jury de Presse at the International Festival of contemporary mime - MIMOS, Périgueux (France)
- The Golden Mask, a theatrical award in Russia

Source (edited): "http://en.wikipedia.org/wiki/DEREVO"

Kokoro Dance

Kokoro Dance is one of Canada's leading butoh dance troupes. Based in Vancouver, British Columbia, it was founded in 1986 by artistic directors Barbara Bourget and Japanese Canadian Jay Hirabayashi. They have performed across Canada, in the United States, and abroad.

As is characteristic of butoh dance, they often perform naked, shaved heads, and covered in white body make-up. They perform an annual dance at Vancouver's clothing-optional Wreck Beach.
Source (edited): "http://en.wikipedia.org/wiki/Kokoro_Dance"

Sankai Juku

Sankai Juku (山海塾) is an internationally known butoh dance troupe. Co-founded by Amagatsu Ushio in 1975, they are touring worldwide, performing and teaching. As of 2010, Sankai Juku had performed in 43 countries and visited more than 700 cities.

Amagatsu Ushio

Amagatsu continues as the group's director, choreographer, designer and dancer. He trained in classical as well as modern dance before he developed his own "second-generation" Butoh style. He maintains that "butoh is a dialogue with the gravity," while other dance forms tend to revel in escape from gravity. He sees his dance, in contrast, is based on "sympathizing or synchronizing" with gravity.

Sankai Juku and butoh

Butoh's source is the Japanese avantgarde of the 1960s, a period when Japan struggled with the lingering effects of the atomic bomb detonations at Hiroshima and Nagasaki that ended World War II. Originally called "ankoku butoh," or "dance of darkness," the medium created a space for the intensely grotesque and perverse on the stage. Amagatsu's work exhibits the conventional tensions of butoh and envelops them in a mood of emotional stillness. "Sankai Juku" means "studio by the mountain and the sea" and implies the serenity and calm which is characteristic of the work.

Sankai Juku's dancers have, like other tipical Butoh dancers, shaved heads and bodies covered in white powder. They may be costumed, partially costumed, or almost unclothed. Rarely wearing typical "street" clothing onstage, they sometimes wear long skirt-like garments.

The all-male company's work is performed by as few as six dancers eschewing the movements typical of modern or other dance forms. The performances are characterized by slow, mesmerizing passages, often using repetition and incorporating the whole body, sometimes focusing only on the feet or fingers. Sometimes minuscule movement or no movement is discernible and one is presented a meditative vision of statuesque postures or groupings. Occasionally recognizable emotive postures and gestures are used, notably contorted body shapes and facial expressions conveying ecstasy and perhaps more often, pain and silent "shrieks." Frequently, ritualized formal patterns are employed, smoothly evolving or abruptly fractured into quick, sharp, seemingly disjointed sequences whose symbolism or "meanings" are obscure.

Music and sound effects are employed, often repetitiously, and range from dynamic drumming to jazz, natural sounds such as wind, sirens, etc., to electronic music and sounds so soft as to be barely perceptible - and periods of silence. Spare scenic backgrounds, delicately nuanced lighting and arresting props (in "Kinkan Shonen," a live peacock) add to the ethereal nature of their performances.

Tours and debuts

In 1980, Sankai Juku performed for the first time in Europe, playing at the Nancy International Festival in France and that same year at the Avignon Festival. The company remained in Europe for four years, appearing at the Edinburgh Festival, the Madrid International Festival and the International Cervantino Festival. In 1984 the group made North American debuts at the Toronto International Festival and the Los Angeles Olympic Arts Festival. They subsequently toured extensively in North America and Canada.

Since 1990 Sankai Juku has performed in Singapore, Hong Kong, Taiwan, Korea, Indonesia, and Malaysia. They made a Russian and East European tour in 1998.

Tragic episode

A signature motif in a work titled "Sholiba" involves a performer suspended upside down. This feat is performed outside, with the dancers suspended from the front of buildings. On September 10, 1985, in Seattle, Washington, one of the original members of the troupe, Yoshiuki Takada, participating in a demonstration, died in a hospital shortly after his supporting rope gave way. Sponsors said that the rigging had been successfully tested with sandbags just before the performance and that this act had been performed "hundreds of times." The troupe continued the upside down hangings, notably outside the National Theatre in Washington, D.C. on May 12, 1986, and in their performances of "Kinkan Shonen" at the Kennedy Center for the Performing Arts in February 2008.

Repertoire and commissions

While keeping early works in their repertoire, the group has premiered new pieces, one almost every other year. Théâtre de la Ville in Paris, France has commissioned 13 of their productions, indicated by "TVP" below.

Among their works are:
- "AMAGATSU SHO (HOMAGE TO ANCIENT DOLLS)" (1977)
- "KINKAN SHONEN" (1978)
- "SHOLIBA" (1979)
- "BAKKI" (1981)
- "JOMON SHO" - TVP (1982)
- "NETSU NO KATACHI" - TVP (1984)
- "UNETSU - The Egg stands out of Curiosity" - TVP (1986)
- "SHIJIMA - The Darkness Calms down in Space" - TVP (1988)
- "OMOTE - The Grazed Surface" - TVP (1991)
- "YURAGI - In a Space of Perpetual Motion" - TVP (1993)
- "HIYOMEKI - Within A Gentle Viblation and Agitation" - TVP (1995)
- "HIBIKI - Resonance from Far Away" - TVP (1998)
- "KAGEMI - Beyond The Metaphors of Mirrors" - TVP (2000)
- "UTSURI - Virtual Garden" - TVP (2003)
- "KINKAN SHONEN - The Kumquat Seed" (premiere 1978 / recreation 2005)

- "TOKI - A Moment in the Weave Time" - TVP (2005)
- "UTSUSHI" (2008) a collage of from previous works
- "TOBARI - As if in an inexhaustible flux" - TVP (2008)
- "Kara・Mi - Two Flows" - TVP (2010)

Awards and recognition

- In 1982, "Kinkan Shonen" was awarded the Grand Prix of Belgrade International Theatre Festival.
- In 1982, "Kinkan Shonen" was awarded the TZ Rose at the Munich Theatre Festival.
- In February 2002, "HIBIKI" won the 26th Laurence Olivier Award for Best New Dance Production.
- In 2007, "TOKI" received "Grand Prix of the 6th The Asahi Performing Arts Awards" and Sankai Juku received "Kirin Special Grant for Dance."

Books and photo collections

- Photo collection "SANKAI JUKU" Photographer: Guy Delahaye, Actes Sud, 2000
- Photo collection "LUNA" diredted and choreographed by Ushio Amagatsu, feat. Sayoko Yamaguchi and Sankai juku.
- Photo collection "THE EGG STANDS OUT OF CURIOSITY" diredted and choreographed by Ushio Amagatsu

Source (edited): "http://en.wikipedia.org/wiki/Sankai_Juku"

A Strange Thing To Say

"A Strange Thing to Say" (EP) is part 1 of the trilogy of "A Triptychon of GHOSTS (or: El Sexorcismo de Anna-Varney Cantodea)". This is the first Sopor recording since 2003's Es Reiten... to not be produced by John A. Rivers. Instead, Patrick Damiani, of the band Rome, has co-produced the record.

The EP comes in 3 different versions; a digiBook version featuring a music video, a special Fan package and a 12" vinyl edition featuring a bonus track. The digibook edition comes with a 96-pages booklet and various other goodies, while the Vinyl comes with an A4 12-pages booklet and the option to have a personal message signed by Anna Varney herself.

Track listing

All songs by Anna-Varney Cantodea, unless otherwise noted.

1. A Strange Thing To Say (9:43)
2. Polishing Silver (5:11)
3. The Urine Song (4:18)
4. Stains of You (4:16)
5. 20,000 Leagues under the SEA (or: The History Of STEAMPUNK ... - abridged) (6:39)
6. Oh, Chimney Sweep (Bonus Track) (3:38)
7. A Strange Thing To Say (Music Video; filmed by Raven Digitalis) (10:00)
8. Too - Tha - Loo (Vinyl edition bonus track) (1:24)

Personnel

- Patrick Damiani: Co-Producer
- Anna-Varney Cantodea

References

Source (edited): "http://en.wikipedia.org/wiki/A_Strange_Thing_To_Say"

Dead Lovers' Sarabande (Face One)

"Dead Lovers' Sarabande" (Face One) is the fourth album by darkwave band Sopor Aeternus & the Ensemble of Shadows, and was released in 1999. It is the first concept album by the band, and the first of a two-album suite detailing the mourning of a lover who has recently passed. *(Face One)* was also the first Sopor Aeternus album to be released in multiple formats, including a double vinyl edition and an A5-sized boxed set edition; both were limited pressings, of 500 and 3,000 copies, respectively. It was also the first to be promoted with an accompanying video.

Overview

"Dead Lovers' Sarabande", as a whole, is a transitory death suite detailing the unnamed protagonist's mourning of her lover and her desire to rejoin him in the afterlife. Major recurring themes in the work include loneliness and the dreadful feeling of loss when someone dear dies. The story of the first part centers around Cantodea assisting her husband in committing suicide; although he is said to be suffering, the exact cause is not mentioned. In "Hades "Pluton"", she attempts to make a deal with otherworldly beings in order to recover her husband but refuses it eventually. Anna-Varney Cantodea later admitted that *"Dead Lovers' Sarabande "* was dedicated to, but not about, the late Rozz Williams, former frontman of deathrock band Christian Death.

Musically, a shift was made towards folk music and chamber pieces, with more prominent passages for string instruments. For the first time, live brass and woodwinds players were used instead of synthesized instruments; the leap to organic strings occurred on *The inexperienced Spiral Traveller*. Whereas previous albums contained some wall of sound production techniques, *(Face One)* was more intimate and featured minimalist arrangements. Songs also became more drone-like, with the use of pedal tones and repeated melodies carried across several instruments; this is most notable on opener "Across the Bridge" and the album's longest piece, "The Sleeper". "Hades "Pluton"" is based on the rhythm of the Roky Erickson, "Night of the Vampire".

"Dead Lovers' Sarabande" (Face One) was re-released on CD with newly packaged artwork in 2004.

Track listing

All songs written by Anna-Varney Cantodea.

1. "Across the Bridge" – 4:44
2. "On Satur(n)days we used to sleep" – 8:58
3. "Hades "Pluton"" – 6:12
4. "Sieh', mein Geliebter, hier hab' ich Gift" – 6:22
5. "Ich wollte hinaus in den Garten" – 8:32
6. "Gebet: an die glücklichen Eroberer" – 1:59
7. "Lament/Totenklage" – 8:18
8. "The Sleeper (by Edgar Allan Poe)" – 11:57
9. "Die Knochenblume" – 1:05
10. "Inschrift/Epitaph" – 3:27
11. "All good Things are Eleven" – 2:49

Personnel

- Katrin Ebert: Violin
- Martin Höfert: Cello
- Johannes Knirsch: Double bass
- Eric Santie-Laa: Cor anglais
- Peter Hergert: Trumpet, trombone
- Eugene de la Fontaine: Tuba, oboe
- Martin Hoffman: Guitars
- Anna-Varney Cantodea: Vocals, all other instruments and programming

Source (edited): "http://en.wikipedia.org/wiki/Dead_Lovers%27_Sarabande_(Face_One)"

Dead Lovers' Sarabande (Face Two)

"Dead Lovers' Sarabande" (Face Two) is the fifth album by darkwave band Sopor Aeternus & the Ensemble of Shadows, and was released in 1999. It is the second of a two-album suite detailing the mourning of a lover who has recently passed. Like *(Face One)*, *(Face Two)* was also released in multiple formats, including a double vinyl edition and an A5-sized boxed set edition; both were limited pressings, of 500 and 3,000 copies, respectively.

Overview

"Dead Lovers' Sarabande", as a whole, is a transitory death suite detailing the unnamed protagonist's mourning of her lover and her desire to rejoin him in the afterlife. Major recurring themes in the work include euthanasia, necrophilia, decay and loneliness. In *(Face Two)*, the protagonist seems to have accepted the fact that her lover is dead and they will no longer share the same life they have led. She decides to continue loving him as she always have, despite his memory haunting her. She concludes by admitting that "it's easier to love the dead" and that she would truly be alone if Love was considered everything in life, rather than Death or Loneliness. Anna-Varney Cantodea later admitted that *"Dead Lovers' Sarabande"* was dedicated to, but not about, the late Rozz Williams, former frontman of deathrock band Christian Death.

The album retains the focus on folk music and chamber pieces presented by *(Face One)*, but transplants many of the string instruments for brass arrangements. Electric guitar is featured on "If Loneliness was all", for the first time since *"Todeswunsch - Sous le soleil de Saturne"*. The influence of drone music is still present on songs like "Procession/Funeral March". "Va(r)nitas, vanitas..." contains elements of "Feralia Genetalia" from *"Voyager" - The Jugglers of Jusa*. As a subtle joke, Cantodea referenced her own name in the song title, effectively translating it as "Varney, vanity... (...all is vanity)."

"Dead Lovers' Sarabande" (Face Two) was re-released on CD with newly packaged artwork in 2004.

Track listing

All songs written by Anna-Varney Cantodea, unless otherwise noted.

1. "Abschied (orig. words & lyrics by NICO)" (Christa Päffgen) – 7:01
2. "The Dog Burial" – 1:15
3. "The House is empty now" – 2:54
4. "No-one is there" – 6:41
5. "Procession/Funeral March" – 6:44
6. "Va(r)nitas, vanitas... (...omnia vanitas)" – 9:05
7. "The Hourglass" – 2:22
8. "Transfiguration" – 5:20
9. "Has he come to test me?" – 2:09
10. "If Loneliness was all" – 8:40
11. "Daffodils" – 7:22

Personnel

- Katrin Ebert: Violin
- Martin Höfert: Cello
- Johannes Knirsch: Double bass
- Eric Santie-Laa: Cor anglais
- Doreena Gor: Bassoon
- Michael Schmeißer: Trumpet
- Carsten Weilnau: Trombone
- Eugene de la Fontaine: Tuba, oboe
- Thomas Langer: Guitars
- Anna-Varney Cantodea: Vocals, all other instruments and programming

Source (edited): "http://en.wikipedia.org/wiki/Dead_Lovers%27_Sarabande_(Face_Two)"

Ehjeh Ascher Ehjeh

Ehjeh Ascher Ehjeh (Hebrew: אהיה אשר אהיה; "I am that I am") is the first EP by Sopor Aeternus & the Ensemble of Shadows, and was released in 1995 as a companion to the album *"Todeswunsch - Sous le soleil de Saturne"*. Only 3,000 copies were pressed. The title of the EP is the response God gave to Moses when he was asked for his name, as seen in the Bible (Exodus 3:14.) The cover painting is a detail of *Saint Jerome Writing* by Michelangelo Merisi da Caravaggio.

The EP contains three songs featured on *"Todeswunsch"* stripped of their backing tracks, bookended by the new song "anima" and a demo recording of "Tanz der Grausamkeit". "anima" began the recurring theme of sexual re-orientation in Anna-Varney Cantodea's lyrics, evident in the concluding line: *"My true self is female how could I ever doubt..."*

Ehjeh Ascher Ehjeh was re-released alongside *"Voyager - The Jugglers of Jusa"* and the demo tape *Es reiten die Toten so schnell...* for the first time as part of the rarities box set *Like a Corpse standing in Desperation*, due to costly prices for cheap copies of the EP sold on eBay.

Track listing

All songs by Anna-Varney Cantodea.
1. "anima I" – 0:50
2. "Shadowsphere II" – 2:31
3. "Saltatio Crudelitatis" – 5:37
4. "freitod-Phantasien" – 3:33
5. "anima II" – 3:05
6. "Tanz der Grausamkeit (demo)" – 5:27

Personnel

- Varney: All vocals, instruments and programming

Source (edited): "http://en.wikipedia.org/wiki/Ehjeh_Ascher_Ehjeh"

Es reiten die Toten so schnell

Not to be confused with the Sopor Aeternus demo tape, Es reiten die Toten so schnell...

"Es reiten die Toten so schnell" (or: the Vampyre sucking at his own Vein) (German: *"The Dead ride so fast"*; usually referred to as **"Es reiten die Toten so schnell"**) is the seventh album by darkwave act Sopor Aeternus and the Ensemble of Shadows, and was released in 2003. A double vinyl edition and an A5-sized boxed set edition was released, in limited quantities of 666 and 1,999 copies, respectively. The double vinyl edition came with a poster, t-shirt, postcards, communion wafers and "authenticated" graveyard soil.

Overview

For *"Es reiten die Toten so schnell"*, Anna-Varney Cantodea went back to her demo tape of the same name and re-recorded all of its songs; the first seven tracks of this album consist of the demo tape in its original sequence. The rest of the album features re-recordings of the bonus tracks that were included on the first Sopor Aeternus album, *"...Ich töte mich jedesmal aufs Neue, doch ich bin unsterblich, und ich erstehe wieder auf; in einer Vision des Untergangs..."*, along with a handful of new songs. "Birth - Fiendish Figuration", Sopor Aeternus' signature song from their first album, appears again in its fourth incarnation on a record. The original version of "Reprise" was a spoken word piece featuring a line from the bridge of "Dead Souls".

John A. Rivers, producer for Swell Maps, Dead Can Dance and Love and Rockets, was brought in to oversee production on *"Es reiten..."*. The album was recorded in England, as opposed to Sopor Aeternus' home country of Germany.

Track listing

All songs written, composed and arranged by Anna-Varney Cantodea.
1. "Omen Sinistrum" – 2:46
2. "Dead Souls" – 7:04
3. "Stake of my Soul" – 3:01
4. "Beautiful Thorn" – 5:14
5. "Baptisma" – 6:37
6. "The Feast of Blood" – 3:35
7. "Sopor Fratrem Mortis Est" – 5:33
8. "The Dreadful Mirror" – 5:53
9. "Reprise" – 3:41
10. "Birth - Fiendish Figuration" – 2:52
11. "Penance & Pain" – 4:26
12. "Holy Water Moonlight" – 5:11
13. "Infant" – 0:51
14. "Über den Fluss" – 2:04
15. "Dark Delight" – 6:43

Personnel

- Chris Wilson: Violin
- Elizabeth Tollington: Cello
- Marcus Cornall: Double bass, electric bass
- Tonia Price: Clarinet
- Eugene de la Fontaine: Oboe
- Eric Santie-Laa: Cor anglais
- Doreena Gor: Bassoon
- James Cunningham: Trumpet
- Julian Turner: Trombone
- Joan Sweet: Tuba
- Paul Brook: Drums
- Anna-Varney Cantodea: Vocals, all other instruments and programming

Source (edited): "http://en.wikipedia.org/wiki/Es_reiten_die_Toten_so_schnell"

Es reiten die Toten so schnell...

Not to be confused with the later Sopor Aeternus album, "Es reiten die Toten so schnell" (or: the Vampyre sucking at his own Vein).

Es reiten die Toten so schnell... (German: *The Dead ride so fast...*) is the first demo tape by darkwave band Sopor Aeternus & the Ensemble of Shadows'. *Es reiten...* was issued in a hand-numbered limited edition of 50 copies in 1989. A further two demo tapes, *Rufus* and *Till Time and Times Are Done*, have not yet been released in any format. All three have been referred to as the "Undead-Trilogy".

Overview

Es reiten... was recorded by Anna-Varney Cantodea (then known simply as Varney) and her then-companion Holger; they would come together only once a month to record and edit the tape until its conclusion. Cantodea thanked Holger greatly for his help in creating *Es reiten...*, especially since the two of them were not financially successful at the time.

The music and lyrics provided an introduction to what would be seen as the "signature" sound of Sopor Aeternus: Renaissance- and Baroque-inspired music, accompanied by Cantodea's voice and a drum machine. As was the case with her early recordings, Cantodea would only record the vocals once, and would not edit the performance later. "Reprise" consists solely of a spoken line during the bridge of "Dead Souls". The majority of the lyrical content in this early phase was vampirism, with songs such as "Stake of my Soul" and "The Feast of Blood" being prime examples. Cantodea discussed the subject matter in 1992:

"We recorded Es reiten die Toten so schnell... *to express the deep bounds towards, well, to our beings suffering their immortal lives in eternal darkness. The lyrics of the Undead-Trilogy allude to vampires only at first sight for they are a symbol of tragedy, damnation and all of that..."*

The material from *Es reiten...* would be entirely re-arranged and re-recorded for the later album *"Es reiten die Toten so schnell" (or: the Vampyre sucking at his own Vein)*, while the original release would be re-issued alongside *"Voyager - The Jugglers of Jusa"* and *Ehjeh Ascher Ehjeh* in the rarities box set *Like a Corpse standing in Desperation*. The original demo appears on the first disc of the collection in a remastered format, removing tape hiss and improving dynamics; the facsimile cassette included in the set contains the songs as originally mixed.

Track listing

All songs written by Sopor Aeternus. Both sides contain the same songs.
1. "Omen Sinistum" – 2:15
2. "Dead Souls" – 6:41
3. "Stake of my Soul" – 1:14
4. "Beautiful Thorn" – 5:09
5. "Baptisma" – 5:01
6. "The Feast of Blood" – 4:07
7. "Sopor Fratrem Mortis Est" – 4:55
8. "Reprise" – 0:16 *(unlisted track)*

Personnel

- Varney: vocals and instruments
- Holger: instruments

Source (edited): "http://en.wikipedia.org/wiki/Es_reiten_die_Toten_so_schnell..."

Flowers in Formaldehyde

"Flowers in Formaldehyde" is the second EP by darkwave band Sopor Aeternus & the Ensemble of Shadows, and was released in 2004 as a companion to the album *"La Chambre D'Echo" - Where the dead Birds sing*. Only 2,000 CDs and 700 LPs were pressed.

Originally announced as *The Adventures of Ms Penny Dreadful*, "Flowers" featured four new songs, two instrumentals of songs from *"La Chambre D'Echo"* and an extensive remix of "Do you know my Name ?" from Sopor Aeternus' first album, *"...Ich töte mich jedesmal aufs Neue, doch ich bin unsterblich, und ich erstehe wieder auf; in einer Vision des Untergangs..."*. The first half of the EP remains some of Sopor Aeternus' most pop-oriented work yet.

"Flowers in Formaldehyde" was re-issued the following year as part of the rarities box set *Like a Corpse standing in Desperation*. Apocalyptic Vision explained that extensive counterfeiting of the EP was cause for its inclusion in the set.

Track listing

All songs written by Anna-Varney Cantodea.
1. "In an Hour Darkly" – 4:58
2. "The Conqueror Worm (by Edgar Allan Poe)" – 3:28
3. "Minnesang" – 3:36
4. "Von der Einfalt" – 1:40
5. "Hearse-shaped Basins of Darkest Matter (instrumental)" – 3:39
6. "Leeches & Deception (instrumental)" – 6:59
7. "Extract from: The Voices of the Dead" – 0:58
8. "Do you know my Name ? / What has happened while we slept ?" – 5:06

Personnel

- Susannah Simmons: Violin
- Elizabeth Tollington: Cello
- Miriam Hughes: Flute
- Tonia Price: Clarinet
- Andrew Pettitt: Oboe
- Doreena Gor: Bassoon
- Tim Barber: Trumpet
- Julian Turner: Trombone
- Anthony Bartley: Tuba
- Paul Brook: Drums
- Anna-Varney Cantodea: Vocals, all other instruments and programming

Source (edited): "http://en.wikipedia.org/wiki/Flowers_in_Formaldehyde"

Ich töte mich...

"...Ich töte mich jedesmal aufs Neue, doch ich bin unsterblich, und ich erstehe wieder auf; in einer Vision des Untergangs..." (German: *"...I kill myself every time again, but I am immortal, and I rise again; in a vision of Doom.."*; usually referred to as *"...Ich töte mich..."*) is the debut album by darkwave band Sopor Aeternus & the Ensemble of Shadows, and was released in 1994. The original pressing had no title, though the "...Ich töte mich..." line was printed in blackletter on the back cover; later editions identified the printed sentence as the official title. Originally released as a limited edition of 1,000, the album has been re-released at least three times.

Overview

"...Ich töte mich..." consists of baroque-

tinged neo-medieval music and is heavily punctuated by drum machines and pipe organs. Much of the instrumentation is synthesized due to a low budget; the album features guitar performed by Gerrit Fischer on its final tracks. Sopor Aeternus would not return to prominent synthesizer use until 2004's *"La Chambre D'Echo" - Where the dead Birds sing*. *"...Ich töte mich..."* features several elements of the musical project's traditional musicality, including the use of brass and woodwinds throughout. "Birth - Fiendish Figuration" would go on to be re-recorded at least three more times on later albums, while "Tanz der Grausamkeit" would be re-recorded as "Saltatio Crudelitas" for *"Todeswunsch - Sous le soleil de Saturne"* and the raucous "Do you know my Name?" would receive equal treatment on *"Flowers in Formaldehyde"*.

In 1999, *"...Ich töte mich..."* was re-released with slightly different artwork and seven bonus tracks, including a couple of demos; "Baptisma", "Beautiful Thorn" and the second half of "The Feast of Blood" (from *Es reiten die Toten so schnell...*) were re-issued on this pressing. All of the bonus songs were later re-recorded for the 2003 album *"Es reiten die Toten so schnell" (or: the Vampyre sucking at his own Vein)*.

The album has since been re-issued twice with different artwork; once in 2004, and again in 2008. The artwork for the 2004 edition stresses that the full recording consists of demos, and the accompanying press release from Apocalyptic Vision suggested to purchase *"...Ich töte mich..."* after one is already acquainted with Sopor Aeternus' music. This press release was later removed from the website. From the 2004 edition onward, all songs had their subtitles removed.

Track listing

All songs by Anna-Varney Cantodea, unless otherwise noted.

1. "Travel on Breath (the Breath of the World)" – 3:46
2. "Falling into different Flesh" – 5:14
3. "Birth - Fiendish Figuration" – 5:00
4. "Tanz der Grausamkeit" – 5:37
5. "Im Garten des Nichts (a secret Light in the Garden of my Void)" – 10:51
6. "Time stands still... (...but stops for no-one)" – 8:42
7. "Do you know my Name ? (Falling... - reprise)" – 4:17

Bonus tracks (later pressings)

8. "Penance & Pain" – 6:21
9. "Holy Water Moonlight" – 5:49
10. "Beautiful Thorn" – 5:00
11. "The Feast of Blood" – 2:37
12. "Dark Delight (dedicated to Victor Bertrand. Performed live without audience... - for the Dead.)" – 4:46
13. "Baptisma" – 4:45
14. "Birth - Fiendish Figuration ("The inner Hell" - orig. demo)" – 5:28

Personnel

- Gerrit Fischer: Guitar on "Time stands still..." and "Do you know my Name ?"
- Varney: Vocals, all other instruments and programming

Source (edited): "http://en.wikipedia.org/wiki/Ich_t%C3%B6te_mich..."

La Chambre D'Echo

"La Chambre D'Echo" - Where the dead Birds sing is the eighth album by darkwave band Sopor Aeternus & the Ensemble of Shadows, and was released in 2004. *"La Chambre D'Echo"* saw the return of synthesizers and drum machines, while still focusing on chamber music-inspired darkwave music. John A. Rivers returned to produce the album alongside Anna-Varney Cantodea. An accompanying EP, *"Flowers in Formaldehyde"*, was released later that year. The album was introduced and promoted via a promotional video.

Overview

"La Chambre D'Echo" was heavily inspired by Der Narrenturm, an old Austrian hospital and psychiatric ward that has since become a museum of diseases, mutations and abnormalities of the human body. As a result, the lyrical focus is that of hospitals and medical care in general. The album artwork, in part, features Cantodea transforming into a large worm-like creature, reminiscent of the artwork for Marilyn Manson's *Antichrist Superstar*.

The album featured prevalent use of synthesizers and drum machines, reflecting Sopor Aeternus' first album, *"...Ich töte mich jedesmal aufs Neue, doch ich bin unsterblich, und ich erstehe wieder auf; in einer Vision des Untergangs..."*.

The packaging for *"La Chambre D'Echo"* is elaborate and extensive. The standard edition comes inside a 128-page, A4-sized book containing photography by Joachim Luetke, as well as handwritten lyrics provided by Cantodea. The photoshoot for the album was taken inside and around Der Narrenturm. The boxed set edition came in a linen-bound box and also included bookmarks, postcards, a translation guide and a pamphlet advertising Der Narrenturm; the included book was enclosed and sealed in an envelope. Curiously, the cover of the vinyl edition featured an image taken for the previous album, *"Es reiten die Toten so schnell" (or: the Vampyre sucking at his own Vein)*. The vinyl edition features its own abridged version of the book as well as a poster. A postcard was included with the album, offering fans the chance to pre-order *"Flowers in Formaldehyde"*.

Track listing

All songs written by Anna-Varney Cantodea.

1. "The Encoded Cloister" – 4:44
2. "Backbone Practise" – 6:00
3. "Idleness & Consequence" – 5:08
4. "Beyond the Wall of Sleep" – 3:31
5. "Imhotep (Schwarzer Drache mischt einen Sturm)" – 4:48
6. "Hearse-shaped Basins of darkest Matter" – 3:57
7. "Interlude - The Quiet Earth" – 8:34
8. "We have a Dog to exercise" – 5:50

9. "The Lion's Promise" – 4:52
10. "Leeches & Deception" – 9:11
11. "The Skeletal Garden" – 4:05
12. "Feed the Birds" – 0:21
13. "Consolatrix has left the Building" – 4:34
14. "Day of the Dead" – 6:23

Personnel
- Chris Wilson: Violin
- Susannah Simmons: Violin
- Liz Hanks: Cello
- Miriam Hughes: Flute
- Tonia Price: Clarinet
- Andrew Pettitt: Oboe
- Doreena Gor: Bassoon
- James Cunningham: Trumpet
- Tim Barber: Trumpet
- Julian Turner: Trombone
- Anthony Bartley: Tuba
- Paul Brook: Drums
- Anna-Varney Cantodea: Vocals, all other instruments and programming

Source (edited): "http://en.wikipedia.org/wiki/La_Chambre_D%27Echo"

Like a Corpse standing in Desperation

Like a Corpse standing in Desperation is the title of a career-spanning rarities box set by darkwave band Sopor Aeternus & the Ensemble of Shadows that was released in 2005. The recordings span fifteen years of "original demos, rarities & documented failures." Re-issued for the first time are the out-of-print EP *Ehjeh Ascher Ehjeh* and remix album *"Voyager - The Jugglers of Jusa"*, along with the never before heard demo tape *Es reiten die Toten so schnell...* and the extensively bootlegged *"Flowers in Formaldehyde"*.

Overview

Like a Corpse... was created in response to the high prices fans would have to pay on eBay for bootlegged copies of out of print EPs and albums. John A. Rivers, who personally oversaw the remastering of the first six Sopor Aeternus albums, as well as the two to follow (2003's *"Es reiten die Toten so schnell"* (or: the Vampyre sucking at his own Vein)* and 2004's *"La Chambre D'Echo" - Where the dead Birds sing*) supervised and remastered the contents of this box set. The set also included the concurrently released single, *"The Goat" / "The Bells have stopped ringing"*.

Barring the aforementioned single and demo tape, four previously unreleased songs were included: "White Body", "Watch your Step", "As Fire kissed the Echo Twins" and "The Widow's Dream"; the last of which is based on the Rozz Williams song "A Widow's Dream". "White Body" is sourced from one of the two still-unreleased demo tapes by Sopor Aeternus.

The box set contains three CDs, packaged in their own hardcover booklet; the book also includes liner notes by Anna-Varney Cantodea herself, as well as "the only interview/publication that I have kept over the years." Also included is a working facsimile of the original cassette tape for *Es reiten die Toten so schnell...*, complete with both original and re-packaged artwork (on both sides); two DVDs (one in NTSC format, the other in PAL) containing five Sopor videos; a T-shirt, a poster, a sticker, patches, buttons, a decorative attachment for a funeral wreath and a signed and numbered certificate of authenticity.

Of interest to some listeners are the two different mixes of the demo tape material. The original demo appears on the first disc of the collection in a re-mastered format, removing tape hiss and improving dynamics; the cassette included in the set contains the songs as originally mixed. The songs from *Jekura - Deep the Eternal Forest* and *Ehjeh Ascher Ehjeh* were also remastered in a similar fashion. Also of note are the two versions of the video for "Deep the eternal Forest"; one, with Anna-Varney Cantodea in black robes, is found on the NTSC DVD; while the other, with Cantodea in white robes, is found on the PAL DVD. The menus of each disc are different as well.

Track listing

All songs written by Anna-Varney Cantodea, unless otherwise noted.

Disc 1: *Original DEMO Recordings*
Es reiten die Toten so schnell...
1. "Omen Sinistrum (original demo)" – 2:15
2. "Dead Souls (original demo)" – 6:41
3. "Stake of my Soul (original demo)" – 1:14
4. "Beautiful Thorn (original demo)" – 5:09
5. "Baptisma (original demo)" – 5:01
6. "The Feast of Blood (original demo)" – 4:07
7. "Sopor Fratrem Mortis Est (original demo)" – 4:55
8. "Reprise (original demo)" – 0:16
9. "White Body (previously unreleased demo, 1992)" – 3:13

Jekura - Deep the Eternal Forest
10. "Diô N'arâp (The unability within Time)" (Ozzy Osbourne, Tony Iommi, Geezer Butler, Bill Ward) – 3:10
11. "Tabor C'âlan O'itanâ (My Womb is barren, but I can conceive)" (Ozzy Osbourne, Tony Iommi, Geezer Butler, Bill Ward) – 7:10
12. "Deep the eternal Forest" – 1:46
13. "Watch your Step (previously unreleased demo, 1994)" – 3:37
14. "Introduction - The Termite People" – 6:45

Ehjeh Ascher Ehjeh
15. "Anima I" – 0:50
16. "Shadowsphere II" – 2:31
17. "Saltatio Crudelitatis" – 5:37
18. "Freitod-Phantasien" – 3:33
19. "Anima II" – 3:05
20. "Tanz der Grausamkeit (recorded on the 28th of October 1993)" – 5:27
21. "As Fire kissed the Echo Twins (previously unreleased demo, 1994)" – 1:49

Disc 2: *"Voyager - The Jugglers of Jusa"*
1. "The inexperienced Spiral Traveller *a fragment* II" – 5:07
2. "Ein freundliches Wort... (...hat meine Seele berührt.) (defined and

fragile)" – 5:10
2. "Memalon II" – 7:25
3. "The Innocence of Devils: "Alone" (E. A. Poe)" – 6:27
4. "Modela est" (Ralf Hütter, Karl Bartos, Emil Schult) – 4:35
5. "Birth (instr.)" – 2:49
6. "Feralia Genitalia (Arrival of the Jugglers)" – 6:30
7. "Menuetto" – 1:26
8. "Saturn-Impressionen (Jusa, Jusa)" – 2:48
9. "May I kiss your Wound ? (Saturn:Orion)" – 6:05
10. "Alone II" – 6:55
11. "The inexperienced Spiral Traveller *a fragment* II (instr.)" – 5:07
12. "The Widow's Dream - fragment (previously unreleased demo, 1999)" – 1:48

"The Goat" / "The Bells have stopped ringing"

1. "The Goat (previously unreleased Outtake, 2000)" – 4:11
2. "The Bells have stopped ringing (previously unreleased, 2000) – 5:05

Disc 3: "Flowers in Formaldehyde"

1. "In an Hour darkly" – 4:58
2. "The Conqueror Worm (by Edgar Allan Poe)" – 3:28
3. "Minnesang" – 3:36

4. "Von der Einfalt" – 1:40
5. "Hearse-shaped Basins of darkest Matter (instrumental)" – 3:39
6. "Leeches & Deception (instrumental)" – 6:59
7. "Extract from: The Voices of the Dead" – 0:58
8. "Do you know my Name ? / What has happened while we slept ?" – 5:06
9. ""La Chambre D'Echo" album trailer (enhanced track)" – 0:42

Cassette: *Es reiten die Toten so schnell...*

Both sides contain the same material.
1. "Omen Sinistum" – 2:15
2. "Dead Souls" – 6:41
3. "Stake of my Soul" – 1:14
4. "Beautiful Thorn" – 5:09
5. "Baptisma" – 5:01
6. "The Feast of Blood" – 4:07
7. "Sopor Fratrem Mortis Est" – 4:55
8. "Reprise" – 0:16

DVD: *SOPOR*

1. "The Goat" – 4:11
2. "...And Bringer of Sadness" – 6:45
3. "Deep the eternal Forest" – 1:46
4. "The Dog Burial" – 1:15
5. "The Bells have stopped ringing" – 5:05

Personnel

Es reiten die Toten so schnell...
- Varney: vocals and instruments
- Holger: instruments

Ehjeh Ascher Ehjeh, Jekura - Deep the Eternal Forest **and all outtakes**
- Varney: All vocals, instruments and programming

"Voyager - The Jugglers of Jusa"
- Una Fallada: Violin
- Matthias Eder: Cello
- Gerrit Fischer: Guitar
- Constanze Spengler: Lute
- Anna-Varney Cantodea: Vocals, all other instruments and programming

"Flowers in Formaldehyde"
- Susannah Simmons: Violin
- Elizabeth Tollington: Cello
- Miriam Hughes: Flute
- Tonia Price: Clarinet
- Andrew Pettitt: Oboe
- Doreena Gor: Bassoon
- Tim Barber: Trumpet
- Julian Turner: Trombone
- Anthony Bartley: Tuba
- Paul Brook: Drums
- Anna-Varney Cantodea: Vocals, all other instruments and programming

Source (edited): "http://en.wikipedia.org/wiki/Like_a_Corpse_standing_in_Desperation"

Sanatorium Altrosa

Sanatorium Altrosa (Musical Therapy for spiritual Dysfunction) is the second remix album by darkwave band Sopor Aeternus & the Ensemble of Shadows, and was released in 2008. It was released as a companion to *Les Fleurs du Mal - Die Blumen des Bösen*, released the previous year, and primarily features alternate versions of songs from that album. Only 999 copies of both the standard and limited editions of the album were pressed. Like its predecessor, *Sanatorium Altrosa* was promoted by video.

The standard edition came in a 52-page hardcover book. The limited edition, known as the "Bag to the Roots Edition", also included *Sanatorium Altrosa* as a double vinyl and a cassette tape; the album *Les Fleurs du Mal* on cassette tape; a t-shirt; a condom and a signed certificate of authenticity. All of the included items were packaged in a Sopor-emblazoned tote bag.

Track listing

All songs by Anna-Varney Cantodea, unless otherwise noted.
1. Consider this: the true Meaning of Love (instr.) – 5:41
2. Architecture II – 7:23
3. Shave, if you love me (remix) – 6:47
4. La Mort d'Arthur (instr.) – 3:00
5. Consider this (orig. version) – 5:37
6. The Conqueror Worm II (instr.) – 3:48
7. In der Palästra (instr.) – 7:09
8. Collision - You May Lie on Your Back, If You Want To ... Even Close Your Eyes to Sleep – 9:45
9. Les Fleurs du Mal (instr.) – 5:15
10. Bitter Sweet (instr.) (Brian Ferry, Andy Mackay) – 5:32
11. Consider this: the true Meaning of Love – 5:39

Personnel

- Naomi Koop: Violin
- Susannah Simmons: Violin
- Liz Hanks: Cello
- Miriam Hughes: Flute
- Andrew Piper: Clarinet
- Mike Davis: Oboe, cor anglais
- Doreena Gor: Bassoon
- Daniel Robson: Trumpet
- Fenton Bragg: Trombone
- Eugene de la Fontaine: Tuba
- Bert Eerie: Drums
- Terence Bat: Drums
- Paul Rothwell: Tenor

- Edward Bellamy: Choirboy
- George Bellamy: Choirboy
- Ian Lewis: Choirboy
- Mark Williams: Choirboy
- Matthew Watson: Choirboy
- Sam Swallow: Choirboy
- Choir of the Collegiate Church of St. Mary of Warwick: Vocals, backing vocals
- Anna-Varney Cantodea: Vocals, all other instruments and programming

Source (edited): "http://en.wikipedia.org/wiki/Sanatorium_Altrosa"

Songs from the Inverted Womb

"Songs from the inverted Womb" is the darkwave band Sopor Aeternus & the Ensemble of Shadows' sixth album, released in 2000. The album is dedicated to the "memory and resurrection" of Little Seven, a boy who died "at the age of six"; *"inverted Womb"* was recorded in an attempt to resurrect (at least) the memory of the boy. A double vinyl edition and a CD boxed set were also released in limited quantities of 666 and 3,000 copies, respectively.

Overview

"Songs from the inverted Womb" builds on the chamber music-inspired sound of the *"Dead Lovers' Sarabande"* albums by adding more conventional song structures and by adding a live drummer. With even more expressive arrangements and enhanced songwriting, *"inverted Womb"* shares many properties with progressive rock. Two songs from previous albums were re-recorded: "May I kiss your Wound ?", from *"The inexperienced Spiral Traveller"* appears in a new arrangement; while "Résumé... -" is a dramatic reworking of "Time stands still... (...but stops for no-one)" from Sopor Aeternus' first album, *"...Ich töte mich jedesmal aufs Neue, doch ich bin unsterblich, und ich erstehe wieder auf; in einer Vision des Untergangs..."*.

As the album is dedicated to "Little Seven", much of the lyrics revolves around finding and caring for the dead boy, as well as other dead children; most of the lyrical imagery revolves around familial plots in small towns in the Middle Ages. "Saturn devouring his Children" deals with necrophagia (the act of eating a corpse), while "There was a Country by the Sea" is an epic tale of finding a boy in a foreign land who has built a catacomb underneath his house; the boy explains to the protagonist that he was able to seal away his mother's bones using "jet-black granules" "piled up in a certain, specific form", but he remains ever vigilant in the tomb so that she will not return to life.

"Résumé... -" was used by Bam Margera in two of his films: *Haggard: The Movie* and *CKY3*; "Eldorado" also made an appearance in *CKY3*. Though not publicly mentioned by Cantodea or Apocalyptic Vision, the inclusion of "Résumé... -" on the *Haggard* soundtrack indicates that permission was granted for use of the two songs.

"Songs from the inverted Womb" was re-released on CD with newly packaged artwork in 2004.

Track listing

All songs written by Anna-Varney Cantodea.

1. "Introduction: Something Wicked this Way comes..." – 4:42
2. "Tales from the inverted Womb" – 4:48
3. "Do you know about the Water of Life?" – 4:49
4. "...And Bringer of Sadness" – 6:45
5. "Résumé... -" – 8:28
6. "Totes Kind / Little dead Boy" – 7:18
7. "May I kiss your Wound ?" – 7:00
8. "Saturn devouring his Children" – 7:02
9. "There was a Country by the Sea" – 12:03
10. "Little velveteen Knight" – 5:52
11. "Eldorado (by Edgar Allan Poe)" – 3:42

Personnel

- Katrin Ebert: Violin
- Martin Höfert: Cello
- Johannes Knirsch: Double bass
- Jutta Sinsel: Clarinet, oboe
- Guido Spitz: Bassoon, contrabassoon
- Alexander Gröb: Trumpet
- Carsten Weilnau: Trombone
- Eugene de la Fontaine: Tuba
- Simon-Tobias Ostheim: Drums, percussion
- Anna-Varney Cantodea: Vocals, all other instruments and programming

Source (edited): "http://en.wikipedia.org/wiki/Songs_from_the_Inverted_Womb"

Sopor Æternus & the Ensemble of Shadows

Sopor Aeternus & The Ensemble of Shadows (Latin: "Eternal Sleep"; often referred to as **Sopor Aeternus** or **Sopor**) is a darkwave musical project based in Frankfurt founded in 1989 by **Anna-Varney Cantodea**. Since the project's beginnings, Anna-Varney's music has gained notoriety for being extremely personalized, melancholic and pessimistic, drawing on a number of different musical and visual styles.

Anna-Varney Cantodea

The *Symbol of Jusa*, as seen on all Sopor Aeternus albums. The symbol represents a connection between the Roman deities Jupiter and Saturn.

Despite years of media attention in Europe, not much is known about Cantodea and her personal life. All known information has been attained from interviews and publications in print. What is established is that Anna-Varney Cantodea is a non-operative trans woman, and has decided to remain as such, citing "spiritual conflict" if gender reassignment surgery is performed. Her name comes from the common name Anna, as well as the Latin word *cantodea*, meaning "female singer". Cantodea had been using the pseudonym Varney prior to 1997, with that name coming from the Victorian Gothic horror story *Varney the Vampire or The Feast of Blood*.

In several interviews, Cantodea has stated that she spent nearly three decades of her life in extreme states of depression, despair and loneliness, brought on by a number of experiences and illnesses in her past. Reportedly, Cantodea suffered beatings at the hands of her parents and peers in school. At the age of six, she was subject to an out-of-body experience whilst under sedation due during a tonsillectomy. By twelve, Anna had started becoming suicidal, and in her adulthood, she had an ailment with cancer-like symptoms, nearly causing her to go blind. These events led to her discovery of the "Ensemble of Shadows"; a group of spirits that Cantodea has said came to her in dreams and provided musical inspiration. The appearance of these otherworldly spirits provided the name for the musical project.

Cantodea seems to be voluntarily isolated, as she has spoken of fear, disgust, or sadness when in the presence of most individuals. She has stated that she does not perform live "in front of humans." Despite this, she currently seems to be acquainted with the pagan and occult author Raven Digitalis, who is one of the "managers" of the official Sopor Aeternus MySpace profile. She has an affinity for author Edgar Allan Poe, recreating his poems through song on several occasions; and is also an avid supporter of several activist philosophies, including euthanasia, LGBT rights, veganism and vegetarianism. Cantodea is a very spiritual person, with devotion placed on the Roman deity Saturn. Saturn's astrological symbol is combined with that of Jupiter's to create the *Symbol of Jusa*, an icon created by Cantodea that reflects her spirituality and has become an insignia for herself and her music. Much of the artwork presented in Varney's albums include astrological imagery.

History

Birth: 1989–1995

Sopor Aeternus & the Ensemble of Shadows was founded by Anna-Varney Cantodea (then known as Varney) and Holger in 1989 and started out as a neue deutsche todeskunst musical project. The two had met in Frankfurt, Germany, in a Goth club called Negativ. The two had met on one of Cantodea's rare outings into the public world. Cantodea and Holger worked together with what little money they had to purchase musical equipment and recorded three demo tapes: *Es reiten die Toten so schnell...*, *Rufus* and *Till Time and Times Are Done*. The three demos were recorded between 1989 and 1992, with *Es reiten...* being the only publicly released cassette. They are collectively referred to as "Blut der schwarzen Rose" (German: "Blood of the Black Rose") or "The Undead-Trilogy". Shortly after the cassettes were created, Holger left Sopor Aeternus.

In 1994, Varney was able to sign with Apocalyptic Vision to release her first album, *"...Ich töte mich jedesmal aufs Neue, doch ich bin unsterblich, und ich erstehe wieder auf; in einer Vision des Untergangs..."* The album, like the demo tapes before it, showcased darkwave music with a neo-classical bent, punctuated by Varney's tortured voice and the recurring imagery of death, despair and vampires. It is unknown if Varney received financial assistance to produce the record.

Renaissance: 1995–2003

Sopor Aeternus' second album, *"Todeswunsch - Sous le soleil de Saturne"*, was an abrupt change in direction. While the album retained qualities of darkwave music, the album was stripped of its heavy use of synthesizers and drum machines and was replaced by a more organic and melancholic approach, resembling music from the Renaissance and Baroque periods. A companion EP, *Ehjeh Ascher Ehjeh*, was released later that year. Varney would also record four songs for an Apocalyptic Vision compilation, *Jekura - Deep the Eternal Forest*; two of the songs appeared under the pseudonym **White Onyx Elephants**.

Sopor's third album, *The inexperienced Spiral Traveller (aus dem Schoß der Hölle ward geboren die Totensonne)*, was released in 1997 alongside a remix album, *"Voyager - The Jugglers of Jusa"*. The two albums became famous for publicly being denounced by Varney as *"the worst album[s] I have ever recorded."* It was around this time that Varney changed her name to Anna-Varney Cantodea; Anna being a common female name, and *cantodea*, the Latin word for "female singer".

1999 saw the double concept album, *"Dead Lovers' Sarabande"*; a project dedicated to the memory of Christian Death frontman Rozz Williams. *"Dead Lovers' Sarabande"* chronicled a nameless protagonist's seemingly futile quest to re-unite with her deceased lover. The album was released in two parts throughout the year, and was the first to be released on vinyl as well as on CD. The following year saw Sopor's sixth album, *"Songs from the inverted Womb"*.

The Goddess: 2003

2003 saw a second rebirth for Sopor Aeternus, both on record and in life. Producer John A. Rivers, known mostly for his work with Swell Maps, Dead Can Dance and Love and Rockets, was brought aboard to produce the seventh album, *"Es reiten die Toten so schnell" (or: the Vampyre sucking at his own Vein)*. The record coupled Rivers' cavernous, wall of sound production techniques with material re-recorded from Sopor's demo tapes with great success, breathing new life into the project. Rivers would go on to produce all new Sopor Aeternus albums.

During the following year, the first six Sopor albums were remastered by Rivers and repackaged with wholly new artwork as a lead up to their eighth album *"La Chambre D'Echo" - Where the dead Birds sing*. Where *Es reiten* started to re-introduce synthesizers into the group's sound, *La Chambre D'Echo* became the first album in a decade to prominently feature synthesizers and drum machines, in a nod to Sopor's first recordings. The companion EP *"Flowers in Formaldehyde"*, as well as the career-spanning rarities box set *Like a Corpse standing in Desperation*, followed.

Around this time, Cantodea became more engaging with her fans; first, by crossdressing heavily (starting with a photoshoot for 2003's *Es reiten...*,) appearing more and more feminine each time. Cantodea re-imagined herself as "The Goddess", adopting the persona of a well-mannered yet sassy widow. With her newfound personification, her online presence grew exponentially with an official website, which included personal messages to fans. Her official website would eventually prove to be a prelude to a foray onto MySpace, where she promotes new releases, sells records and infrequently blogs. Her ninth album, *Les Fleurs du Mal - Die Blumen des Bösen*, fully embraced the feminine persona.

At the beginning of 2010, the band's official ReverbNation page was updated with the status "... is currently in seclusion ... - writing beautiful new music(k).". Later on in the year, Anna Varney began posting blogs on the band's official Vampire Freaks page. The blogs outlined the details of various personal issues and also mentioned the upcoming Trilogy of albums. It was later revealed in a blog entitled "DEATH", that the Trilogy is "A Triptychon of Ghosts". On September 26 it was announced through the official website and the band's Vampire Freaks page that *A Strange Thing To Say* was released on 2010 as the "opening chapter" to "A Triptychon of Ghosts". Sopor Aeternus will be releasing the next album, *Have You Seen This Ghost?* on April 26th, 2011.

Musical characteristics

Cantodea, photographed in 2000 for *"Songs from the inverted Womb"*

The sound of Sopor Aeternus is rooted in renaissance and baroque music, with main use of brass instruments, woodwinds, strings, pipe organs, bells, and guitars. While earlier works used drum machines, later albums feature live percussion. Cantodea's work has shown a progression towards livelier arrangements and more wall of sound production, compared to earlier works; more recent albums have also employed a slightly more mainstream sound, incorporating electronic and slight gothic rock sentiments. Though considered by genre a darkwave band, Cantodea has stated that she ignores this notion and simply creates *"...-music for dead children [and otherwise wounded souls], that is all."* On several occasions, Cantodea has re-recorded and recycled elements from previous songs; other times, motifs are used; the most notable example is "Birth - Fiendish Figuration", which has been re-recorded at least four times.

Cantodea has clearly stated that she creates her music about herself, solely for herself. Major themes include death, unrequited love, karmatic pain, loneliness, sadness, spirituality and failure; more recently, Cantodea has featured occultism, sexuality and romance into her lyrics. A strong recurring theme is transexuality, especially the removal of male genitalia. Several albums feature Cantodea nude with a vagina (which was edited in in post-production.) Many allusions to spirituality and Roman deities appear in her lyrics; aside from Jupiter and Saturn, Morpheus, Hades, Uranus and Charon have been addressed by name. Other supernatural figures mentioned include the Sister of Self-Destruction, the Goat, the Old Man and the Lord of the Darkest Side.

Discography

Demo tapes

The three demo tapes are often referred to as "Blut der schwarzen Rose" or "The Undead-Trilogy". Only the first has been released.
- *Es reiten die Toten so schnell...* (1989)
- *Rufus* (1992)
- *Till Time and Times Are Done* (1992)

Studio albums
- *"...Ich töte mich jedesmal aufs Neue, doch ich bin unsterblich, und ich erstehe wieder auf; in einer Vision des Untergangs..."* (1994)
- *"Todeswunsch - Sous le soleil de Saturne"* (1995)
- *The inexperienced Spiral Traveller (aus dem Schoß der Hölle ward ge-*

- boren die Totensonne) (1997)
- "Dead Lovers' Sarabande" (Face One) (1999)
- "Dead Lovers' Sarabande" (Face Two) (1999)
- "Songs from the inverted Womb" (2000)
- "Es reiten die Toten so schnell" (or: the Vampyre sucking at his own Vein) (2003)
- "La Chambre D'Echo" - Where the dead Birds sing (2004)
- Les Fleurs du Mal - Die Blumen des Bösen (2007)
- Have you seen this Ghost? (2011)

EPs and remix albums (Sister Albums)
- Ehjeh Ascher Ehjeh (1995)
- "Voyager - The Jugglers of Jusa" (1997)
- "Flowers in Formaldehyde" (2004)
- Sanatorium Altrosa (Musical Therapy for spiritual Dysfunction) (2008)
- A Triptychon of Ghosts (Part One) - A Strange Thing to say (2010)

Singles
- "The Goat" / "The Bells have stopped ringing" (2005)
- "In der Palästra" (2007)

Other releases
- Jekura - Deep the Eternal Forest (1995) – a compilation featuring four songs by Sopor Aeternus
- Nenia C'alladhan (2002) – a self-titled side project with Constance Fröhling
- Like a Corpse standing in Desperation (2005) – a boxed set of rarities and hard-to-find albums
- The Goat and Other Re-Animated Bodies (2009) - DVD of previously released videos

Videography

Sopor Aeternus has released promotional videos to accompany their music. Most videos are noticeably abstract, with several layers of footage composited to create a distinctly blurred effect. "Deep the Eternal Forest" received two versions: one with Varney in white robes, and the second with Varney in black robes. The first six listed here were included as part of the box set *Like a Corpse standing in Desperation*, while "In der Palästra" was included on its own DVD single. All of Sopor Aeternus' videos have been directed by Anna-Varney Cantodea herself.
Source (edited): "http://en.wikipedia.org/wiki/Sopor_%C3%86ternus_%26_the_Ensemble_of_Shadows"

The Inexperienced Spiral Traveller

The inexperienced Spiral Traveller (aus dem Schoß der Hölle ward geboren die Totensonne) (German: "from the Womb of Hell was born the Sun of the Dead") is the third album by darkwave band Sopor Aeternus & the Ensemble of Shadows, and was released in 1997. *The inexperienced Spiral Traveller* continued the Renaissance- and Baroque-inspired sound of *"Todeswunsch - Sous le soleil de Saturne"*, but with tighter arrangements and the re-introduction of drum machines. A limited edition of 3,000 copies was initially available alongside the regular edition, and the album has been re-issued at least twice since.

Overview

The inexperienced Spiral Traveller was the first album to set the sound of Sopor in stone, with its tighter, more expressive arrangements and full utilization of strings and brass. The musical palette was enhanced by the edition of actual violin, cello and lute players, where synthesizers had been previously used. Drum machines were also integrated with the live percussion on several songs, and production values were at their highest yet with full use of studio techniques, as heard on opening track "Sylla'borêal". Despite this, Anna-Varney Cantodea has publicly stated her distaste for the album, stating:
Hmm... Well... Let's put it this way: The inexperienced Spiral Traveller, *has been the worst album I have ever recorded... And after that... It slowly got better.*
Similar comments were made about the accompanying remix album, *"Voyager - The Jugglers of Jusa"*.

The subject matter of the album mainly deals with the isolation brought on by Cantodea's illnesses through life. It has been stated in interviews that one illness nearly blinded her permanently, and much of the imagery of the album comes from that episode. The identity of the "loyal friend" mentioned is unknown (although many fans now believe this reference is primarily to depression), but on the later-released *"La Chambre D'Echo" - Where the dead Birds sing*, Cantodea states that *"this once so loyal friend ..., he's not that welcome anymore."* The song "Birth - Fiendish Figuration" was re-recorded for this album, while "May I kiss your Wound ?" would be re-recorded for *"Songs from the inverted Womb"*.

In 2004, *The inexperienced Spiral Traveller* was re-issued with entirely new artwork, including radically new art and liner notes. The new artwork emulates a tourism package, including a passport and the photographs from the older version encaspulated in Polaroid borders. The back cover also featured a mock advertisement for the Synchro-Box, quoted to be "the best device to travel the continuum".

Track listing

All songs by Anna-Varney Cantodea, unless otherwise noted.

1. "Sylla'borêal (Embracing the Dead prior to the Service)" – 5:05
2. "Question(s) Beyond Terms (Who is confronting the Impossible?)" – 5:44
3. "C'ayllagher a Dom'bhrail (There is no need to remind me)" – 0:58
4. "To a loyal Friend" (anonymous 16th century Italian composition; arr. Sopor Aeternus) – 6:58
5. "Never trust the Obvious (or: The Innocence of Devils)" – 6:52
6. "The inexperienced Spiral Traveller *a fragment*" – 5:08

7. "Memalon" – 7:24
8. "Memories are Haunted Places (Birth - Fiendish Figuration, vers.)" – 5:42
9. "Die Widerspenstigkeit unerwünschter Gedanken" – 2:32
10. "Synchronicity (To Saturn:Orion)" – 0:27
11. "Totenlicht (Infant in the face of Time)" – 6:02
12. "Ein freundliches Wort... (...hat meine Seele berührt.)" – 5:11
13. "Die Toten kehren wieder mit dem Wind" – 2:55
14. "May I kiss your Wound?" – 5:47
15. "Ein gütiges Lächeln auf den Gesichtern der Toten..." – 5:26

Personnel
- Una Fallada: Violin
- Matthias Eder: Cello
- Gerrit Fischer: Guitar
- Constanze Spengler: Lute
- Anna-Varney Cantodea: Vocals, all other instruments and programming

Source (edited): "http://en.wikipedia.org/wiki/The_Inexperienced_Spiral_Traveller"

Todeswunsch

Todeswunsch - Sous le soleil de Saturne (German and French: *"Death wish - Under the sun of Saturn"*) is the second album by darkwave band Sopor Aeternus & the Ensemble of Shadows and was released in 1995. *Todeswunsch* saw a fundamental change in sound, abandoning the heavily-synthesized darkwave music for a sound akin to the Renaissance and neo-Medieval music. A limited pressing of 3,000 CDs was initially available, and the album has been re-released at least three times. An accompanying EP, *Ehjeh Ascher Ehjeh*, was released later that year.

Overview

"Todeswunch" was a major departure from Sopor Aeternus' first album, *"...Ich töte mich jedesmal aufs Neue, doch ich bin unsterblich, und ich erstehe wieder auf; in einer Vision der Untergangs..."*, in that the aggressive synthesized music of the first record was replaced with ornate Renaissance- and Baroque-inspired folk music. Brass, woodwinds and acoustic guitars came to the fore, while drum machines were largely abandoned for varying amounts of hand percussion. Shrill female vocals also resound throughout the album, with most if not all of them provided by Anna-Varney Cantodea herself. The abrupt change in direction provoked mixed reactions from fans.

The album quotes heavily from other works. One example is the title track, which is a darkwave version of Cat Stevens' "I Think I See the Light". "Drama der Geschlechtslosigkeit (part 2)" quotes from "Chim Chim Cher-ee", as featured in *Mary Poppins*, while "Shadowsphere" quotes the bass lines from Black Sabbath's "Under the Sun". "The Devil's Instrument" also quotes lyrics from Rozz Williams' "Mysterium Inquitatis". *"Todeswunsch"* contains the first instance of Cantodea's long-standing interest in Edgar Allan Poe: "Die Bruderschaft des Schmerzes" is a re-telling of his work *Dream-Land*.

"Todeswunsch" would see re-releases in 1999, 2003 and 2008. The album artwork received significant changes for both the 2003 and 2008 editions. The painting on the cover of the original release is a detail of *Death of the Virgin* by Michelangelo Merisi da Caravaggio. The title of "Soror Sui Excidium" was changed to "Soror (Sister of Self-destruction)" for re-releases, and both halves of "Shadowsphere" were indexed into one track on re-issue.

Track listing

All songs by Anna-Varney Cantodea, unless otherwise noted.
1. "Flesh Crucifix (Suffering from Objectivity)" – 1:52
2. "Die Bruderschaft des Schmerzes (Die Unbegreiflichkeit des Dunklen Pfades, den die Kinder Saturns gehen)" – 5:49
3. "Shadowsphere (The Monologue-World and the subconscious Symbols): part one" – 5:02
4. "Shadowsphere (The Monologue-World and the subconscious Symbols): part two" – 2:35
5. "Saltatio Crudelitatis (Tanz der Grausamkeit, vers.)" – 5:47
6. "Just a Song without a Name" – 0:28
7. "Soror Sui Excidium (Geliebte Schwester Selbstzerstörung)" – 4:35
8. "Le Théâtre de la Blessure sacrée" – 2:58
9. "The Devil's Instrument" – 5:18
10. "Todeswunsch (vers.)" (Cat Stevens) – 5:38
11. "Drama der Geschlechtslosigkeit (part 1)" – 2:05
12. "freitod-Phantasien" – 3:23
13. "Drama der Geschlechtslosigkeit (part 2)" – 5:10
14. "Saturn-Impressionen" – 2:47
15. "Somnabulist's secret Bardo-Life (Does the Increase of Pain invite the Absence of Time?)" – 4:17
16. "Not dead but dying" – 5:11
17. "Only the Dead in the Mist" – 5:12
18. "This profane Finality" – 4:35
19. "Cage within a Cage... (...within a Cage within a Cage...)" – 1:59

On later pressings, both parts of "Shadowsphere" would be combined as one track. "Soror Sui Excidium" was renamed "Soror (Sister of Self-destruction)" on later editions.

Personnel
- Gerrit Fischer: Guitar on "Soror Sui Excidium", "Drama der Geschlechtslosigkeit (part 2)" and "Only the Dead in the Mist"
- Varney: Vocals, all other instruments and programming

Source (edited): "http://en.wikipedia.org/wiki/Todeswunsch"

Voyager: The Jugglers of Jusa

Voyager: The Jugglers of Jusa is the first remix album by darkwave band Sopor Aeternus & the Ensemble of Shadows, and was released in 1997. It was released as a companion to *The inexperienced Spiral Traveller (aus dem Schoß der Hölle ward geboren die Totensonne)*, also released that year, and primarily features alternate versions of songs from that album. Only 3,000 copies of the album were pressed.

Overview

Like the earlier EP *Ehjeh Ascher Ehjeh*, "Voyager" consists of remixed versions of songs accompanied by some newer songs. Most of the remixed songs have had either their backing tracks removed, or had extra percussion and drum machines added. "Never trust the Obvious" receives two remixes: "The Innocence of Devils: Alone", which contains a recitation of author Edgar Allan Poe's *Alone*; and "Alone II", an extended version. The signature piece "Birth - Fiendish Figuration" is also featured as an instrumental; a remix of "Saturn-Impressionen" from *"Todeswunsch - Sous le soleil de Saturne"* also appears on this album.

The newer songs include "Modela est", a cover version of Kraftwerk's "Das Model" ("The Model"), sung in Latin; and "Feralia Genitalia", another ode to transgenderism as Anna-Varney Cantodea describes her "genitals rotting off" and her transformation into a woman.

"Voyager" - The Jugglers of Jusa was re-released alongside *Ehjeh Ascher Ehjeh* and the demo tape *Es reiten die Toten so schnell...* as part of the rarities box set *Like a Corpse standing in Desperation*, due to costly prices for cheap copies of the album being sold on eBay. In the liner notes of the box set, Anna-Varney announces her outright hatred for *"Voyager"* by opening its section of liner notes with:

"... - oh dear. What good thing could I possibly say about this most horrible piece of crap?!"

Similar comments were made about *The inexperienced Spiral Traveller*. Cantodea, in the same essay, expresses her wishes to re-record the album at a future point. So far, only "May I kiss your Wound?" has been re-recorded (for *"Songs from the inverted Womb"*), while elements of "Feralia Genetalia" were re-used for "Va(r)nitas, vanitas... (...omnia vanitas)" on *"Dead Lovers' Sarabande" (Face Two)*.

Track listing

All songs by Anna-Varney Cantodea, unless otherwise noted.

1. "The inexperienced Spiral Traveller *a fragment* II" – 5:07
2. "Ein freundliches Wort... (...hat meine Seele berührt.) (defined and fragile)" – 5:10
3. "Memalon II" – 7:25
4. "The Innocence of Devils: "Alone" (E. A. Poe)" – 6:27
5. "Modela est" (Ralf Hütter, Karl Bartos, Emil Schult) – 4:35
6. "Birth (instr.)" – 2:49
7. "Feralia Genitalia (Arrival of the Jugglers)" – 6:30
8. "Menuetto" – 1:26
9. "Saturn-Impressionen (Jusa, Jusa)" – 2:48
10. "May I kiss your Wound? (Saturn:Orion)" – 6:05
11. "Alone II" – 6:55
12. "The inexperienced Spiral Traveller *a fragment* II (instr.)" – 5:07

Personnel

- Una Fallada: Violin
- Matthias Eder: Cello
- Gerrit Fischer: Guitar
- Constanze Spengler: Lute
- Anna-Varney Cantodea: Vocals, all other instruments and programming

Source (edited): "http://en.wikipedia.org/wiki/Voyager:_The_Jugglers_of_Jusa"